"Think vegan, gluten-free baking means settling for something less-than-delicious? Think again! *Decadent Gluten-Free Vegan Baking* proves that you can be ingredient-conscious without compromising on fun or flavor."

—NATALIE SLATER, author of *Bake and Destroy*

"Whether you are craving a cookie, a cupcake, a donut or a scone, just pour a tall glass of ice cold almond milk and get your taste buds ready for the foods you thought you'd have to go without."

—JONI MARIE NEWMAN, author of *The Best Veggie Burgers on the Planet*, *Fusion Food in the Vegan Kitchen* and many more

"Cara's debut cookbook proves that eating vegan and gluten-free can be fun! Her allergy-friendly takes on old favorites are an absolute delight."

—ALLYSON KRAMER, author of *Great Gluten-Free Vegan Eats* and *Sweet Eats for All*

Decadent Gluten-Free vegan Baking

Delicious Gluten-, Egg- and Dairy-Free Treats and Sweets

Cara Reed

creator of the popular site
ForkandBeans.com

PAGE STREET
PUBLISHING CO.

PAGE STREET
PUBLISHING CO.

First published in 2014 by
Page Street Publishing Co.
27 Congress Street, Suite 103
Salem, MA 01970
www.pagestreetpublishing.com

Distributed by Macmillan; sales in Canada by The Canadian Manda Group.

18 17 16   3 4 5

ISBN-13: 978-1-62414-071-6
ISBN-10: 1-62414-071-8

Library of Congress Control Number: 2014930248

Cover and book design by Page Street Publishing Co.
Photography by Celine Steen

Printed and bound in China

Page Street is proud to be a member of 1% for the Planet. Members donate one percent of their sales to one or more of the over 1,500 environmental and sustainability charities across the globe who participate in this program.

contents

INTRODUCTION

Unlike cooking, baking has an entire science to it. It takes a certain amount of knowledge to understand how many eggs a recipe needs in order to give it a beautiful rise, how much fat requires a baked good to taste a certain way, and even what the right amount of liquid is needed without weighing it down. Take away the gluten, eggs and dairy, now we are talking about a whole new set of rules to abide by. This is why the task of initially learning how to bake gluten-free and vegan can be so overwhelming. I can recall the first six months of adjusting to this new science. They were some of the most frustrating times ever! With trash bags full of "rocks," which were supposed to resemble breads and muffins, that crumbled with the slightest touch, I was ready to give up altogether.

Maybe that is you right now. You are ready to throw in your towel and apron and cry into the big bag of gluten-free flour mix in your pantry. Maybe you are completely new to baking without gluten, eggs and dairy and have no idea where to start. I completely understand that feeling. Or maybe you have a few years of experience under your belt and are looking for new recipes to add to your collection. Wherever you are at I guarantee you that, like it was for me, persistence and tenacity will lead you to a better understanding of this world of gluten-free vegan baking. Anything is possible if you are willing to commit (after all, I am writing this cookbook—me, the girl who years prior, would sit on her kitchen floor sobbing because she just baked four different batches of cookies that all tasted like doo-doo). Don't be shy, grab ahold of my hand and believe me when I say you can so do this! Make sure to check out my Resources section (page 165) for tips, tricks and basic recipes used throughout the book. This will be a guide for you to understand how to substitute certain ingredients in my recipes that you are unable to consume.

chapter 1

CHILDHOOD FAVORITES

Growing up as a little girl, I had two favorite activities: watching TV and eating. A really good day was when I was able to combine both activities. It's true that I had developed some rather bad habits as a kid. It's why I ended up on the chubbier side.

As I have grown older, wiser and more knowledgeable about how to properly feed my body (I know now that a bag of Doritos and a can of Coke is nowhere near a perfectly balanced meal), I have in return watched my waistline shrink. But the old saying is still true: You can take the girl out of the junk food, but you can't take the junk food out of the girl. Okay, so I made that one up.

Despite the fact that I treat my body entirely differently as an adult doesn't mean that I can no longer enjoy foods that bring me back to my childhood, like a homemade Oreo cookie dunked in a cold glass of almond milk. Put that apron on, sister (or brother), and let's get baking. Who wants homemade Pop-Tarts or better yet cinnamon sugar churros with a homemade chocolate dipping sauce? I had a feeling you would like that . . .

GIRL SCOUT COOKIES

SAMOAS

Despite the fact that they always come in 2nd behind the triumphant Thin Mints, Samoas will always remain my favorite Girl Scout cookie. A crispy cookie bottom coated with chocolate and topped with caramel and coconut is in my opinion neck and neck with chocolate and mint. One of my favorite ways to eat Samoas is by breaking them apart and throwing them into a big bowl of nondairy ice cream.

MAKES APPROXIMATELY 30 COOKIES

FOR THE COOKIE BASE
1 ¼ c/206 g Cara's All-Purpose Blend (page 166)
3 Tbsp/45 ml maple syrup
2 Tbsp/28 g non-hydrogenated shortening
2 Tbsp/28 g vegan butter
1 Tbsp/15 ml nondairy milk
¾ tsp baking powder
½ tsp salt

FOR THE CHOCOLATE COATING
2 c/352 g nondairy chocolate chips, melted
1 Tbsp/15 ml non-hydrogenated shortening or coconut oil, melted

FOR CARAMEL AND COCONUT
Date Caramel Sauce (page 148)
1 ½ c/90 g sweetened shredded coconut, toasted

Preheat oven to 325°F/170°C. Line a baking sheet with parchment paper.

Mix everything for the cookie base together with a fork in a medium bowl until dough begins to form. It might be a bit crumbly; simply place the dough on a piece of parchment paper and gently knead until a smooth ball is formed. Roll between 2 pieces of parchment until ⅛ inch/3 mm. Cut into circles with 2-inch/5-cm cookie cutter. Using a ½-inch/12-mm circle cutter, make a hole in the middle of each cookie.

Bake for 10 to 12 minutes. Allow to fully cool.

Dip each cookie bottom into the melted chocolate and coconut oil. Allow to set on a piece of parchment paper.

Mix together the caramel sauce and coconut in a small bowl. Spoon approximately 1 tablespoon/15 ml of the mixture onto each cookie and spread around so it covers it completely.

Place the leftover melted chocolate in a plastic bag, cut a tiny hole in the corner and drizzle lines on the top. Freeze the cookies for 10 minutes to completely set.

CARA'S TIP: You might have leftover date caramel sauce for this recipe, and you are better for it! Simply place into an airtight jar and store in the refrigerator for up to one week. Drizzle over nondairy ice cream or a slice of pie, or spoon it right out of the jar for a sweet treat.

Thin Mints

One of the main reasons I do what I do is because it gives me so much joy and satisfaction to know that the special people in my life are able to safely enjoy the foods everyone else around them enjoys. The best day of my baking career was when I was able to make these Thin Mints with my (at the time) 7-year-old niece Cambria, who is severely allergic to dairy and eggs. The excitement she got from being able to eat the cookies she sells with her troop was one of the best feelings I have ever experienced.

Makes approximately 30 cookies

1 ¼ c/206 g Cara's All-Purpose Blend (page 166)

¼ c/22 g cocoa powder

3 Tbsp/45 ml maple syrup

3 Tbsp/42 g non-hydrogenated shortening

1 Tbsp/15 ml nondairy milk

2 tsp unsulphured molasses

½ tsp baking powder

½ tsp salt

FOR THE CHOCOLATE COATING

1 c/176 g nondairy chocolate chips

1 Tbsp/14 g non-hydrogenated shortening

½ tsp (or more based on preference) peppermint oil

Preheat oven to 325°F/170°C. Line a baking sheet with parchment paper.

Mix everything but the chocolate coating ingredients together with a fork in a medium bowl until dough begins to form. It might be a bit crumbly; simply place the dough on a piece of parchment paper and gently knead until a smooth ball is formed. Roll between 2 pieces of parchment until ⅛ inch/3 mm. Cut into circles with 2-inch/5-cm cookie cutter.

Bake for 10 to 12 minutes. Allow to fully cool.

Melt the chocolate chips in a microwave-safe bowl. Every 30 seconds, stop and stir, and then heat up again until the chocolate is completely melted. Add shortening and peppermint oil and stir until smooth.

Dip each cookie into the bowl of chocolate and coat. Freeze for 10 minutes until set. Best if kept in fridge or freezer.

Trefoil Cookies

Part butter cookie, part shortbread—this hybrid version of the Trefoil touts a super-crunchy and buttery flavor but is made without all the things that upset your belly.

Makes 24 cookies

8 Tbsp/112 g vegan butter, chilled and cubed

½ c/60 g powdered sugar

½ c/100 g granulated sugar

2 c/330 g Cara's All-Purpose Blend (page 166)

¼ tsp salt

¼ tsp xanthan gum

Coarse sugar (optional) for sprinkling the dough

Preheat oven to 350°F/180°C. Coat a baking sheet with parchment paper.

With an electric mixer, blend the butter and sugars together just until combined. No more than 30 seconds—you do not want too much air to get into the butter.

In a separate bowl, whisk together the flour, salt and xanthan gum until well mixed. Add flour mix into the butter mix with the mixer briefly until just combined. Knead with your hands until smooth. Roll dough out between 2 pieces of parchment paper until ¼-inch/6-mm thick. Cut into desired shape and then place on the baking sheet. Sprinkle each cookie with coarse sugar and freeze for 20 minutes. Bake in the oven for 20 to 25 minutes or until lightly browned, and allow to cool on a wire rack.

Tagalongs

A decadent mountain of fluffy peanut butter smothered in chocolate, these Tagalongs are bursting with deliciousness. Dare I say to chop a bunch of them up and add them to a bowl of nondairy ice cream? Talk about a sugared-up brain freeze!

Makes approximately 30 cookies

1 ¼ c/206 g Cara's All-Purpose Blend (page 166)

3 Tbsp/45 ml maple syrup

2 Tbsp/28 g non-hydrogenated shortening

2 Tbsp/28 g vegan butter

1 Tbsp/15 ml nondairy milk

¾ tsp baking powder

½ tsp salt

FOR THE PEANUT BUTTER FILLING

½ c/129 g peanut butter

6 Tbsp/84 g non-hydrogenated shortening

1 c/120 g powdered sugar

FOR THE CHOCOLATE

2 c/352 g nondairy chocolate chips

2 Tbsp/28 g shortening or coconut oil, solid

Preheat oven to 325°F/170°C. Line a baking sheet with parchment paper.

Mix everything but the filling and chocolate together with a fork in a medium bowl until dough begins to form. It might be a bit crumbly; simply place the dough on a piece of parchment paper and gently knead until a smooth ball is formed. Roll between 2 pieces of parchment until ⅛ inch/3 mm. Cut into circles with 2-inch/5-cm cookie cutter.

Bake for 10 to 12 minutes. Allow to fully cool.

To make the filling

Using an electric mixer, combine peanut butter and shortening until fully mixed. Slowly add the powdered sugar and mix until light and fluffy.

To assemble

Place approximately 1 tablespoon/16 g of peanut butter onto fully cooled cookie. Make a small mountain-like hump.

Freeze cookies with filling for 15 to 20 minutes just so it doesn't melt into the chocolate. Remove from freezer and allow cookies to sit and breathe for a couple of minutes.

To make the chocolate

Place the nondairy chocolate chips in a microwave-safe bowl. Microwave on high for 2 minutes, but stop every 30 seconds to stir. Once they are almost completely melted (it might not even take the full 2 minutes), mix in the shortening or oil and stir until smooth.

Place a frozen cookie (with peanut butter on it) onto a fork and dip it into the chocolate, bottom-side in first. Using a spoon, coat the top with chocolate until it is fully coated. Place on a piece of parchment paper and complete all cookies. Freeze for 10 minutes just to set.

CARA'S TIP: If you have a nut allergy, simply replace the peanut butter with a homemade or store-bought SunButter for a very comparable cookie.

Pecan Sandies

With one bite of these cookies, you will fall in love all over again. Each nibble contains a beautiful combination of toasty pecans and sweet butter flavor. Dusted with just enough powdered sugar, these are a great cookie fresh out of the oven.

Makes approximately 36 cookies

1 ¼ c/206 g Cara's All-Purpose Blend (page 166)
½ c/60 g toasted pecans, chopped
3 Tbsp/45 ml maple syrup
3 Tbsp/42 g non-hydrogenated shortening
2 Tbsp/28 g vegan butter
1 Tbsp/15 ml nondairy milk
¾ tsp baking powder
½ tsp salt
Powdered sugar for dusting

Preheat oven to 325°F/170°C. Line a baking sheet with parchment paper.

Mix everything together with a fork in a medium bowl until dough begins to form. It might be a bit crumbly; simply place the dough on a piece of parchment paper and gently knead until a smooth ball is formed. Roll between 2 pieces of parchment until ¼ inch/6 mm. Cut into circles with 2-inch/5-cm cookie cutter. Place on baking sheet and lightly dust with powdered sugar.

Bake for 10 to 12 minutes. Allow to fully cool. If desired, dust with more powdered sugar once out of the oven.

Churros with Chocolate Dipping Sauce

Growing up, I didn't really remember places unless they were associated with food. Going to Angels' games? Churros. My dad is rolling his eyes right now at the memory of the endless games he endured with my sister and me always asking the inevitable question: "Can we get a churro now? What about now?" These deep-fried morsels are the perfect once-in-a-while treat to indulge in when you are craving a throwback favorite childhood treat. Rolled in cinnamon and sugar, this dessert becomes all grown up when dipped in my Homemade Chocolate Sauce (page 149).

Makes 12 churro pieces

2 c/480 ml vegetable oil

1 ½ c/248 g Cara's All-Purpose Blend (page 166)

1 ½ tsp/5.5 g baking powder

¼ tsp salt

⅛ tsp nutmeg

½ c/120 ml hot water

3 Tbsp/42 g vegan butter

⅔ c/55 g lightly packed brown sugar

1 Tbsp/12 g ground white chia seeds, soaked in 3 Tbsp/45 ml water

FOR ROLLING

½ c/100 g granulated sugar

1 tsp cinnamon

ADD-ONS

Homemade Chocolate Sauce (page 149)

In a medium saucepan, heat vegetable oil over medium heat to 350°F/180°C. It's important that the oil is not too hot, otherwise the outside of the churro will be crisp but the insides will be gummy.

While the oil is heating up, whisk the flour, powder, salt and nutmeg together in a bowl.

In a medium-sized bowl, pour boiling water over the butter until melted. Add brown sugar and chia soaked in water.

Pour flour mix into the wet mix until thick and combined.

In a shallow bowl, place ½ cup/100 g granulated sugar and 1 tsp cinnamon. You are going to need to have this ready once you retrieve the churros from the hot oil.

Place batter into a pastry bag with a large star tip (if you do not have this, simply place into a large plastic baggie with a cut slightly less than 1-inch/2.5-cm wide in the corner). Squeeze the batter over the oil, creating 2-inch/5-cm pieces. Cook 4 at a time.

Once they are nicely browned (takes 30 seconds—very quick because these are small pieces), remove from oil and gently place into the shallow bowl with cinnamon and sugar. Toss in mixture.

Serve with warmed up Chocolate Sauce for a decadent treat.

Chocolate Sandwich Cookie "Oreos"

It is incredible how true-to-the-real-thing this filling is to the original Oreo cookie. The best part about these cookies is getting to twist each end off to see if you can keep the middle filling intact on one cookie side. Of course, they taste better when dunked in a big glass of ice-cold almond milk.

Makes 12 sandwiches

2 ½ c/413 g Cara's All-Purpose Blend (page 166)

½ c/44 g dark cocoa powder

6 Tbsp/90 ml maple syrup

6 Tbsp/84 g non-hydrogenated shortening

2 Tbsp/30 ml nondairy milk

1 Tbsp/22 g unsulphured molasses

1 tsp baking powder

½ tsp salt

FOR THE FILLING

1 ¼ c/150 g powdered sugar

3 Tbsp/42 g non-hydrogenated shortening

1 Tbsp/15 ml nondairy milk

Preheat oven to 325°F/170°C. Line a baking sheet with parchment paper.

Mix everything but the filling ingredients together with a fork in a medium bowl until dough begins to form. It might be a bit crumbly; simply place the dough on a piece of parchment paper and gently knead until a smooth ball is formed. Roll between 2 pieces of parchment until ¼ inch/6 mm. Cut into circles with 2-inch/5-cm cookie cutter.

Bake for 10 to 12 minutes. Allow to fully cool.

To make the filling

With an electric mixer, combine all of the ingredients until cream becomes thick and smooth (about 2 minutes).

Using a spatula, scrape the cream into a plastic baggie. Make a small slit in one corner and thickly distribute the cream in a circular motion onto one cookie. Gently sandwich another cookie on top.

CHEEZ-IT CRACKERS

Please note that these crackers are so insanely good and taste like actual Cheez-Its that you will not want to share with anyone. I suggest that you make them when you are home alone. That way there is no need to feel shame as you shove each cheesy cracker down your throat.

MAKES 4 DOZEN CRACKERS

DRY

¾ c/124 g Cara's All-Purpose Blend (page 166)

½ tsp xanthan gum

½ tsp salt

WET

1 c/112 g cheddar-flavored shredded vegan cheese

3 Tbsp/42 g vegan butter, softened

1 Tbsp/15 ml ice water

Coarse salt for topping

Preheat the oven to 375°F/190°C.

In a small bowl, whisk together the dry ingredients. In a large bowl, beat the vegan cheese and butter together with an electric mixer until well combined. Slowly add the flour mixture into butter/cheese mix until blended. Add the water and stir in with a rubber spatula until a dough ball forms.

Place the dough on a piece of parchment paper and lightly knead until a smooth ball is made. Divide the dough in half and place one half of the dough in the fridge. In between 2 pieces of parchment paper, roll out the dough with a rolling pin to about a ¼-inch/6-mm thickness. With a pastry cutter (these have squiggly lines that give the fun shape to the cracker) pattern out the shapes of the squares, going horizontally and diagonally.

Using a stainless steel spatula, slowly and gently place each cracker on top of a parchment-lined baking sheet, making sure to space them ½ inch/12 mm apart. This might be the longest part of the process, but you do want to go slowly in order to maintain the shape. Make a little hole in the center of each cracker. Sprinkle the tops with a dash of coarse salt.

Place the baking sheet of crackers in the freezer for 10 minutes while you repeat the same process for the next half of the dough. Bake for 17 to 20 minutes until the edges are lightly browned. Allow to cool on baking sheet.

CARA'S TIP: There is no need to make your crackers look like real Cheez-Its if you don't have the time. You can simply use a small cookie cutter of choice. In my opinion, though, making the crackers look like the real deal does make them taste better (wink).

"Pop-Tarts"

Though not deemed to be a healthy breakfast, Pop-Tarts have been around for years. They are also the perfect on-the-go breakfast item because of how quickly they toast in the oven and how easily they travel with you. These used to be my go-to breakfast choice (thankfully I have realized otherwise since then), but now these homemade tarts make a great dessert or special treat.

Makes 6 "Pop-Tarts"

DRY

3 c/495 g Cara's All-Purpose Blend (page 166)

2 Tbsp/25 g granulated sugar

2 tsp /6.5 g xanthan gum

1 tsp salt

WET

10 Tbsp/140 g vegan butter, chilled and cubed

6 Tbsp/84 g non-hydrogenated shortening

10 Tbsp/150 ml cold water

FOR "EGG" WASH, FULLY MIX TOGETHER

1 tsp cornstarch

1 Tbsp/15 ml water

Whisk the dry ingredients together in a large bowl. Cut the vegan butter and shortening into the flour mixture until the dough forms into small lumps. Add 1 tablespoon/15 ml of chilled water at a time (I only needed 5 total but play it by the tablespoon) until dough is cohesive but not too sticky. Divide in half and roll into balls. Cover and chill in the fridge for at least 30 minutes.

Preheat oven to 350°F/180°C. Line a baking sheet with a piece of parchment paper.

Take one ball of dough out of the fridge and in between 2 sheets of parchment paper, roll to create a rectangle that is 6" x 10"/15 x 25 cm when trimmed and ⅛"/3 mm flat. Using a knife, gently cut out four 3" x 5"/7.5 x 12.5 cm rectangles and place on a parchment-lined baking sheet with a metal spatula. Place 1 tablespoon (20 g for strawberry filling & 13 g for cinnamon sugar filling) of whichever filling you choose (page 27 or 29) on top of each piece, leaving a small border along the edges. Repeat with the next ball of dough. This time, place on top of the pieces with the filling.

Gently take your finger and press down along the edges. Make indentations with a fork to enclose the tart and poke the tops with a fork. Brush tops with "egg" wash and bake 20 to 22 minutes or until lightly browned. Allow to cool and then coat with icing of choice.

Cinnamon & Brown Sugar "Pop-Tarts"

FOR THE CINNAMON SUGAR FILLING
½ c/110 g packed brown sugar
1 Tbsp /10 g Cara's All-Purpose Blend
(page 166)
2 tsp/5 g cinnamon

FOR THE BROWN SUGAR ICING
1 c/120 g powdered sugar
¼ c/36 g lightly packed brown sugar
1 Tbsp/15 ml nondairy milk
½ tsp ground cinnamon
½ tsp vanilla extract

Whisk together the filling ingredients in a small bowl. Fill as described on page 26. Then mix icing ingredients in a bowl and spoon the icing over the baked pastry tarts and allow the "PopTarts" to cool for 5 minutes for the icing to set.

Strawberry Frosted "Pop-Tarts"

FOR THE STRAWBERRY FILLING

6 Tbsp/120 g strawberry jam

2 tsp/6.5 g cornstarch

FOR THE ICING

1 c/120 g powdered sugar

2 tsp/15 ml nondairy milk, more if needed

1 tsp homemade pink food coloring (page 158)

½ tsp vanilla extract

ADD-ONS

Pink Sugar Glitter (page 161)

Combine both ingredients in a small bowl. Fill as described on page 26. Then, mix icing ingredients in a bowl and spoon the icing over the baked pastry tarts. Immediately dust with pink-colored Sugar Glitter and allow the Pop-Tarts to cool for 5 minutes for the icing to set.

Fig Newton Bars

The fig jam in these soft bars adds a nice chewiness to every bite. The best part is crunching down on those tiny fig seeds and getting them stuck in your teeth. Does that sound strange? Well, I am a weird girl with odd attractions. I just really love the pop it makes between my molars. Pop on, player.

Makes 15 bars

4 Tbsp/56 g vegan butter, softened

½ c/72.5 g lightly packed brown sugar

1 Tbsp/7 g flaxseed meal plus 3 Tbsp/45 ml water, thickened for 5 minutes

½ tsp vanilla extract

1 c/165 g Cara's All-Purpose Blend (page 166)

¼ c/30 g buckwheat flour

1 tsp baking powder

¼ tsp salt

5 Tbsp/100 g fig jam

Preheat oven to 350°F/180°C. Line a baking sheet with a piece of parchment paper.

Cream the butter and sugar together with an electric mixer. Add the flaxseed soaked in water and mix. Add vanilla and mix until fully incorporated.

In a small bowl, combine the flours, baking powder and salt. Add slowly to the wet mixture. If you need more flour, add a tablespoon at a time. You want to make sure the dough is not sticky but not dried out either.

Lay 1 piece of parchment paper lightly dusted with flour on the counter. Using ¼ of the dough, knead until it is smooth. Place another piece of parchment paper over the dough and roll out to an approximate 14″ x 6″/35 x 15 cm rectangle, about ¼″/6 mm thick. Cut into 2″ x 2″/5 x 5 cm squares.

Place 1 teaspoon of jam of your choice in the middle of the dough square. Place another square on top. Fold the seams of the sides together. Transfer to parchment paper–lined baking sheet and bake for 15 to 20 minutes or until lightly browned.

Fudge-Striped Cookies

There are two distinct memories I have whenever I think about these cookies: the sound of the plastic tray being pulled out of the bag when diving in for a cookie and the way the fudge felt on my teeth on that first bite. The homemade version is sure to bring you your very own memories (plastic tray not included).

Makes approximately 36 cookies

FOR THE DOUGH

1 c/165 g Cara's All-Purpose Blend (page 166)

¼ c/30 g almond flour

3 Tbsp/45 ml maple syrup

3 Tbsp/42 g non-hydrogenated shortening

2 Tbsp/28 g vegan butter

1 Tbsp/15 ml nondairy milk

¾ tsp baking powder

½ tsp salt

FOR THE CHOCOLATE

1 c/176 g nondairy chocolate chips

1 Tbsp/14 g non-hydrogenated shortening or coconut oil, solid

Preheat oven to 325°F/170°C. Line a baking sheet with parchment paper.

Mix everything together with a fork in a medium bowl until dough begins to form. It might be a bit crumbly; simply place the dough on a piece of parchment paper and gently knead until a smooth ball is formed. Roll between 2 pieces of parchment until ¼ inch/6 mm. Cut into circles with 2-inch/5-cm cookie cutter. Use another ½-inch/12-mm-sized circle and cut out small holes in the middle.

Bake for 10 to 12 minutes. Allow to fully cool. Melt the chocolate chips with the shortening or coconut oil. Dip bottoms into the melted chocolate. Chill in the freezer to set and place the remainder of the chocolate into a plastic baggie or piping bag with a small slit. Make 5 squiggly lines across each cookie. Allow to set either in the freezer or on the counter.

CARA'S TIP: The purpose of the almond flour is to give these cookies a nutty, rich flavor. If you are allergic to almonds or do not have almond flour on hand, just use a total of 1 ¼ cups/206 g of my go-to flour blend.

chapter 2

COOKIES, BARS & BROWNIES

We all have those cookie recipes that have been passed down from generation to generation. You know what I am talking about—those special recipes that never break from tradition within your family. Having food restrictions doesn't mean that you have to stop honoring your heritage. The great thing about this chapter is now you will have new recipes to pass on to your children. Thought chocolate chip cookies were off limits? Not anymore. We are going to get nondairy chocolate in our teeth with an updated version of Grandma's classic recipe. Thought graham crackers were only for gluten lovers? Think again. You are going to wonder how these taste just like actual graham flour. All I have to say about that is welcome to the new world of gluten-, egg- and dairy-free cookies!

Grandma's Chocolate Chip Cookies

I do a yearly Christmas cookie exchange with Brooke of Crackers on the Couch,
a sweet friend of mine whom I met through the awesome world of blogging. Every year she bakes
the original recipe and I do my own gluten-, egg- and dairy-free version. This particular
recipe is my take on her Grandma's chocolate chip cookie, and might I say, they blow
any regular ol' cookie out of the water (or nondairy milk).

Makes approximately 3 dozen cookies

2 c/330 g Cara's All-Purpose Blend (page 166)

1 tsp baking soda

½ tsp salt

1 c/224 g vegan butter, at room temperature

¾ c/165 g packed brown sugar

½ c/100 g granulated sugar

1 ½ tsp vanilla

1 Tbsp/7 g flaxseed meal plus 3 Tbsp/45 ml water

1 ½ c/264 g nondairy chocolate chips

Preheat oven to 375°F/190°C. Line a baking sheet with a piece of parchment paper.

In a medium bowl, whisk together the flour, baking soda and salt. Set aside. In a large bowl, cream the vegan butter and sugars together with an electric mixer until fluffy. Add the vanilla extract and flaxseed soaked in water and beat well. Add the flour mix to the butter mix with a wooden spoon and stir well. Fold in the nondairy chocolate chips.

Roll the cookie dough into a heaping tablespoon ball. Place 2 inches/5 cm apart on the baking sheet and bake for 10 to 12 minutes. Remove cookie sheet from oven and transfer cookies to a cooling rack.

Gingerbread Men

Nothing screams the holidays like a big batch of these cookies filling your home with the amazing aroma of ginger and molasses. This roll-out dough is not only beautifully textured, but it also tastes great straight from the bowl (or so I have heard)...

Makes approximately 2 dozen cookies

½ c/112 g vegan butter

2 ½ c/413 g Cara's All-Purpose Blend (page 166)

1 tsp baking soda

1 tsp ground ginger

½ tsp ground cinnamon

¼ tsp ground cloves

½ c/50 g granulated sugar

½ c/176 g unsulphured molasses

1 Tbsp/7 g flaxseed meal plus 3 Tbsp/45 ml warm water

1 batch Royal Icing (page 158)

In a large bowl, beat the vegan butter with an electric mixer on medium to high speed about 30 seconds or till softened.

Whisk together the flour blend, baking soda, ginger, cinnamon and cloves. Beat half of this flour mix, sugar, molasses and flaxseed soaked in water into the butter. Beat until thoroughly combined. Stir in the remaining flour.

Divide the dough in half and create 2 balls. Place in a bowl, cover and chill for about 3 hours or until easy to handle.

Preheat oven to 375°F/190°C. Line a baking sheet with parchment paper.

On a lightly floured surface, roll each half of dough between 2 pieces of parchment paper into ⅛-inch/3-mm thickness. Create shapes into the dough using the cookie cutter of your choice. Place 1 inch/2.5 cm apart on the prepared cookie sheet.

Bake for 7 to 10 minutes until the edges are lightly browned and firm. Cool on the baking sheet for 1 minute before transferring cookies to a wire rack. Decorate with my Royal Icing.

CARA'S TIP: While you are rolling out a portion of the dough, keep the remainder in the fridge. The longer the dough sits out, the stickier it becomes, causing it to be a hassle to work with. The chilling process allows it to be workable.

The Perfect Sugar Cookie

One of my favorite things to do during any holiday is to spend the entire day making and decorating sugar cookies. I used to be a habitual premade store-bought cookie dough shopper, but when I started having food allergies, I was forced to create a new recipe that would not only carry me throughout the holidays, but could also be passed on to my children's children. I am more than okay if you keep this in your family's tradition as well.

Makes approximately 2 dozen cookies

DRY
1 ¼ c/206 g Cara's All-Purpose Blend (page 166)
2 Tbsp/16 g powdered sugar
½ tsp baking powder
½ tsp salt

WET
3 Tbsp/45 ml maple syrup
2 Tbsp/28 g non-hydrogenated shortening
1 Tbsp/14 g vegan butter
1 Tbsp/15 ml nondairy milk
½ tsp almond extract

ADD-ONS
1 batch Royal Icing (page 158)
A few drops of all-natural coloring (page 158)

Preheat oven to 350°F/180°C. Line a baking sheet with parchment paper.

Whisk together the dry ingredients in a medium bowl. Making a well in the middle, throw in all of the wet ingredients and mix everything together with a fork until dough begins to form. It might be a bit crumbly; simply place the dough on a piece of parchment paper and gently knead until a smooth ball is formed. If it is not smoothing out after it has warmed up between your hands, add 1 teaspoon of nondairy milk at a time until it does. Roll between 2 pieces of parchment until ¼ inch/6 mm. Cut into desired shapes with a cookie cutter.

Bake for 8 to 10 minutes or until lightly browned along the edges (time will vary based on the size of cookie cutter you use). Use Royal Icing mixed with my all-natural food colorings for brightly colored sugar cookies.

CARA'S TIP: My friend Brooke from Crackers on the Couch likes to add ½ teaspoon orange peel zest to her sugar cookies. It really adds a beautiful flavor and is worth trying if you are feeling zesty!

Chocolate Clouds

These remind me a lot of those adorable chocolate crinkle cookies you find around Christmastime, but with a little more crunch. Roll them in powdered sugar before baking and they will really look like they have been kissed by clouds.

Makes 2 dozen cookies

DRY

¾ c/124 g Cara's All-Purpose Blend (page 166)

¼ c/22 g cocoa powder

¼ c/37 g lightly packed brown sugar

¼ c/50 g granulated sugar

½ tsp baking powder

½ tsp baking soda

¼ tsp salt

WET

4 Tbsp/56 g vegan butter, melted

1 Tbsp/7 g flaxseed meal plus 3 Tbsp/ 45 ml warm water

ADD-IN

½ c/88 g nondairy chocolate chips

Preheat oven to 350°F/180°C. Line a baking sheet with parchment paper.

In a large bowl, combine the dry ingredients. Make a well in the middle and throw in the wet ingredients. Stir with a wooden spoon until it is combined, and then fold in the nondairy chocolate chips. Roll the cookie dough by the tablespoon between your hands and place onto the baking sheet. Bake for 8 to 10 minutes (the longer they bake the crunchier they become, so adjust to preference).

CARA'S TIP: These cookies work great with additional add-ins, so get creative! Try ½ cup/60 g chopped hazelnuts for a Nutella version or even give it a sprinkle of 1 cup/45 g shredded coconut and ½ cup/60 g chopped toasted almonds for Almond Joy cookies.

Hot Cocoa Snickerdoodles

A fun twist on the classic snickerdoodle, this version bursts with cinnamon and nutmeg. The perfect melt-in-your-mouth cookie, it will make you believe you are drinking a cup of cocoa. You might even be tempted to cover these with a big batch of nondairy whipped cream. I won't judge.

Makes 2 dozen cookies

DRY

1 ¼ c/206 g Cara's All-Purpose Blend (page 166)

¾ c /150 g granulated sugar

¼ c/22 g cocoa powder

1 tsp cream of tartar

½ tsp baking soda

½ tsp xanthan gum

½ tsp cinnamon

¼ tsp nutmeg

¼ tsp salt

WET

4 Tbsp/56 g vegan butter

4 Tbsp/56 g non-hydrogenated shortening

1 Tbsp/7 g flaxseed meal plus 3 Tbsp/45 ml water, thickened for 5 minutes

1 tsp vanilla extract

ADD-IN

½ c/88 g nondairy chocolate chips

FOR ROLLING

2 Tbsp/26 g granulated sugar

1 tsp cinnamon

Whisk together all of the dry ingredients except the sugar and cocoa powder in a medium bowl. With an electric mixer, beat the vegan butter, shortening and sugar until light and fluffy. Add the cocoa powder and flaxseed soaked in water until fully combined. Stir in vanilla extract. Slowly add the dry ingredients into the butter mix until just combined. Fold in the nondairy chocolate chips. Chill the dough for 30 minutes in the fridge.

Preheat oven to 350°F/180°C. Line a baking sheet with parchment paper.

Mix together the sugar and cinnamon for rolling in a small, shallow dish. For each cookie, roll into a ball with your hands (a heaping tablespoon's worth), roll them in the cinnamon and sugar and place on the baking sheet. Gently flatten with the back of a fork. Bake for 13 to 15 minutes or until edges are lightly browned. Remove from the oven and allow to sit on the baking sheet for 5 minutes before transferring to a cooling rack.

CARA'S TIP: The purpose of the cream of tartar in this recipe is twofold: It imparts a certain tart flavor that is ubiquitous with snickerdoodles, and it reacts quickly with the baking soda while in the oven, which allows for the dough to rise rapidly in the heat and then deflate just as swiftly, imparting that crinkle look we love about these cookies.

Ginger Wafer Thins

These cookies remind me of those cute little thin cookies that you find in the market area of IKEA. The crispy and crunchy texture provides for a perfect dip in a cup of coffee or tea when you need that little something to perk you up midday or after a meal.

Makes 2 dozen wafer cookies

DRY

1 ¼ c/206 g Cara's All-Purpose Blend (page 166)

1 tsp ground ginger

½ tsp cinnamon

½ tsp baking powder

½ tsp salt

Pinch of ground cloves

WET

3 Tbsp/45 ml maple syrup

2 Tbsp/28 g non-hydrogenated shortening

2 Tbsp/30 ml molasses

1 Tbsp/15 ml nondairy milk

ADD-ON

Coarse sugar, for topping

Preheat oven to 325°F/170°C. Line a baking sheet with parchment paper.

Whisk the dry ingredients together in a medium bowl. Combine the wet ingredients into the dry and mix everything together with a fork in a medium bowl until dough begins to form. It might be a bit crumbly; simply place the dough on a piece of parchment paper and gently knead until a smooth ball is formed. If it is still crumbly, add nondairy milk a teaspoon at a time until completely smooth.

Roll between 2 pieces of parchment until ⅛ inch/3 mm. Cut into circles with 2-inch/5-cm cookie cutter. If the dough is too sticky, place in the freezer for 5 to 7 minutes until it firms up enough to work with. Lightly coat tops of cookies with coarse sugar. Transfer cookies to the baking sheet using a metal spatula.

Bake for 10 to 12 minutes. Allow to fully cool.

CARA'S TIP: For a chocolate version, subtract ¼ cup/41 g of the flour blend and replace it with ¼ cup/22 g cocoa powder. Omit the ground cloves.

Old-Fashioned Oatmeal Cranberry Cookies

I'm not sure whether I like this recipe's batter or the actual cookie better. The batter is so good that I secretly hide a stash of it in the freezer in a sealed tub and scoop out a little when I need a cookie dough pick-me-up. I also like to replace the raisins with nondairy chocolate chips, which I am convinced make the cookies so much better!

Makes approximately 2 dozen cookies

DRY

1 ½ c/120 g gluten-free old-fashioned rolled oats

1 c/165 g Cara's All-Purpose Blend (page 166)

½ c/100 g granulated sugar

1 tsp baking powder

½ tsp baking soda

½ tsp salt

WET

4 Tbsp/56 g vegan butter

1 Tbsp/7 g flaxseed meal plus 3 Tbsp/45 ml water

1 tsp vanilla extract

ADD-INS

¾ c/90 g dried cranberries

½ c/60 g walnuts, chopped

Preheat oven to 350°F/180°C. Line a baking sheet with a piece of parchment paper.

In a medium bowl, whisk together all the dry ingredients except for the sugar. In a large bowl, cream the vegan butter and sugar together with an electric mixer until fluffy. Add the flaxseed "egg" and vanilla extract and beat well. Add the dry flour mix to the butter mix with a wooden spoon and stir well. Fold in the dried cranberries and walnuts.

Spoon a heaping tablespoon of the cookie dough onto the baking sheet. Place 2 inches/5 cm apart on the baking sheet and bake for 10 to 12 minutes. Remove cookie sheet from oven and transfer cookies to a cooling rack.

CRANBERRY PISTACHIO BISCOTTI

The combination of sweet and salty is beautifully displayed in this biscotti recipe.
It's one of my favorites, I must say, and it will quickly be yours as well.

MAKES 20 SMALL BISCOTTI

DRY

1 c/165 g Cara's All-Purpose Blend (page 166)

½ c/60 g dried cranberries

¼ c/30 g coarsely chopped unshelled pistachios

1 tsp baking powder

½ tsp xanthan gum

Pinch of salt

WET

1 Tbsp/14 g vegan butter, softened

1 Tbsp/7 g flaxseed meal plus 3 Tbsp/45 ml warm water—thickened for 5 minutes

½ c/100 g granulated sugar

½ tsp vanilla extract

ADD-ON

½ batch Royal Icing (page 158)

Preheat oven to 350°F/180°C. Line a baking sheet with parchment paper.

In a medium bowl, cream the vegan butter, flaxseed soaked in water and sugar with an electric mixer on medium speed until fluffy. Add the vanilla extract. In a small bowl, whisk together the dry ingredients and then add into the butter/ flax "egg" mix. Stir with a wooden spoon until a dough forms. Transfer the dough over to the baking sheet, and with your hands form a loaf approximately 13 x 2 inches/32.5 x 5 cm. Bake for 40 minutes. Allow to cool enough to handle.

With a serrated knife cut the loaf into small slices less than 1 inch/2.5 cm thick on a cutting board. Transfer back onto the baking sheet, cut side down, and bake for another 20 to 25 minutes (flipping over halfway through the baking time) until completely dried out and lightly browned. Cool on a wire rack. Drizzle with Royal Icing.

> **CARA'S TIP:** If your dough is still crumbly, add 1 tablespoon/ 15 ml nondairy milk until smooth.

Gluten-Free Graham Crackers

Have you ever had the craving to stop what you are doing to sit down with a big glass of cold nondairy milk and a handful of graham crackers for dunking? Maybe it's just my kindergarten days that instilled the need in me for a mid-afternoon snack, but these no-graham crackers will bring you back to the days of being 6 years old. Is it nap time yet?

Makes approximately 40 crackers

DRY

2 c/330 g Cara's All-Purpose Blend (page 166)

½ c/72.5 g lightly packed brown sugar

¼ c/40 g teff flour

2 Tbsp/14 g flaxseed meal

1 tsp baking powder

½ tsp salt

¼ tsp cinnamon

WET

5 Tbsp/70 g coconut oil (solid) or non-hydrogenated shortening

½ tsp vanilla extract

3 Tbsp/66 g unsulphured molasses

5 Tbsp/75 ml nondairy milk

Coarse sugar for sprinkling

Preheat oven to 375°F/190°C.

Combine all the dry ingredients in a medium bowl. With a pastry blender or fork, incorporate solid coconut oil into flour until crumbs form. Place the rest of the wet ingredients into the mix until a smooth dough ball is formed.

Divide the dough into 2 balls. Roll out one of the balls onto a piece of parchment until it is ¼ inch/6 mm thick or at desired thickness. Cut into squares by using a pie crust cutter (either a straight edge or one with ridges) or use a square-shaped cookie cutter.

Take a fork and gently poke holes into dough. Sprinkle with coarse sugar, if desired. Bake for 20 minutes or until lightly browned, and allow to cool for 10 minutes.

Chocolate Almond Biscotti

There is nothing like the mild taste of cocoa paired with the awesome crunch of toasted almonds. These crispy cookies are begging to be dunked into your coffee. Why? Well because it's the adult's version of a sophisticated cookie, but of course.

Makes 20 small biscotti

1 Tbsp/14 g vegan butter, softened

1 Tbsp/7 g flaxseed meal plus 3 Tbsp/45 ml warm water—thickened for 5 minutes

½ c/100 g granulated sugar

1 Tbsp/15 ml unsulphured molasses

¼ tsp almond extract

¾ c/124 g Cara's All-Purpose Blend (page 166)

½ c/60 g coarsely chopped toasted almonds

¼ c/22 g cocoa powder

1 tsp baking powder

½ tsp xanthan gum

Pinch of salt

Preheat oven to 350°F/180°C. Line a baking sheet with parchment paper.

In a medium bowl, cream the vegan butter, flaxseed meal soaked in water and sugar with an electric mixer on medium speed until fluffy. Add the molasses and almond extract. In a small bowl, whisk together the flour, almonds, cocoa powder, baking powder, xanthan gum and salt, and then add into the butter/flax "egg" mix. Stir with a wooden spoon until a dough forms. Transfer the dough over to the baking sheet and with your hands form a loaf (approximately 13 x 2 inches/32.5 x 5 cm). Bake for 40 minutes. Allow to cool enough to handle.

With a serrated knife cut the loaf into small slices less than 1 inch/2.5 cm thick on a cutting board. Transfer back onto the baking sheet cut side down, and bake for another 20 to 25 minutes (flipping over halfway through the baking time) until completely dried out and lightly browned. Cool on a wire rack.

CARA'S TIP: If your dough is still crumbly, add 1 tablespoon/ 15 ml nondairy milk until smooth.

The Classic Brownie

A great way to prepare ahead of time for a premade brownie mix is to combine the dry ingredients and store it in an airtight mason jar. When you are ready to whip up a batch, simply add the wet ingredients, throw in a pan and bake. Who needs those store-bought, ready-made boxes anyway?

Makes 12 brownie squares

DRY

1 c/165 g Cara's All-Purpose Blend (page 166)

¼ c/35 g black bean flour

1 ½ c/150 g granulated sugar

¼ c/22 g cocoa powder

½ tsp salt

WET

5 Tbsp/38 g unsweetened applesauce

3 Tbsp/45 g nondairy chocolate chips, melted and cooled

¼ c/60 ml vegetable oil

¼ c/60 ml hot water

ADD-INS

½ c/90 g nondairy chocolate chips

½ c/60 g chopped walnuts

Preheat oven to 350°F/180°C. Grease an 8 x 8-inch/20 x 20-cm square pan.

In a large mixing bowl, combine the dry ingredients. With a wooden spoon, mix the wet ingredients except for the hot water into the dry. The batter will be clumpy and that is okay. Add the hot water and mix until batter becomes smooth and thick enough that when you scoop some up with the spoon and turn it upside down, it won't quickly fall off. Fold in your chocolate chips and walnuts.

Place into brownie pan and bake for 40 to 50 minutes or until a toothpick or knife comes out clean. Allow to sit in the pan and fully cool (at least 30 minutes).

CARA'S TIP: Black bean flour can be found either at your local health food store or on the Internet. If you cannot find it, simply replace with another ½ cup/83 g Cara's All-Purpose Blend (page 166). If you are looking to spruce up this classic recipe, after the brownies cool for 10 minutes, coat Warmed-up Caramel Sauce (page 147) over the top and sprinkle with chopped toasted pecans.

Peanut Butter Cup Bars

I spend most of my time creating recipes over at my website Fork & Beans, and this particular recipe has become a fan favorite. It is so simple to make and so darn delicious! These bars are a part of the cookie exchange I did with my blogger friend Brooke and are translated into their own gluten-, egg- and dairy-free version. These candy-like bars will beg you to utter the classic line, "So this piece of chocolate and slab of peanut butter walk into a bar . . ."

Makes 18 bars

1 ½ c/390 g chunky peanut butter
½ c/120 ml unrefined coconut oil, melted
1 tsp vanilla extract
2 c/240 g powdered sugar
2 c/168 g Gluten-Free Graham Crackers, crushed (page 49)
1 (15-oz [285-g]) bag nondairy chocolate chips, melted

Mix peanut butter, coconut oil, vanilla, sugar and graham crackers together. Press into a parchment-lined 9 x 13-inch/22.5 x 32.5-cm pan. Pour the melted chocolate over the top. Refrigerate for 2 to 3 hours.

Remove from pan with the parchment paper once fully chilled, and slice into squares.

Frozen Blueberry Yogurt Bars

I was beyond ecstatic when I found a nondairy version of Greek yogurt at my local health food store. The options available for those of us who cannot digest certain foods is expanding greatly—we are so lucky! These granola bars are a retake on one of my favorite recipes, which I have had around for years and loved eating for breakfast. I am so happy that I can finally recreate it.

Makes 10 bars

2 ½ c/260 g gluten-free vegan granola of choice
¼ c/56 g vegan butter, melted
3 (6-oz [510-g]) nondairy Greek blueberry yogurts
½ c/70 g fresh blueberries

Preheat oven to 350°F/180°C. Place a piece of parchment paper just enough to cover the bottom of an 8 x 8-inch/20 x 20-cm square pan.

In a large bowl, mix the granola and the melted butter together. Firmly press in bottom of the pan and bake for 10 minutes. Allow to cool fully.

Gently spoon the yogurt over the granola crust. Sprinkle with blueberries and freeze until firm (approximately 2 to 3 hours). Slice in rows of 5 and 2.

Key Lime Cheesecake Bars

This is an homage to my dear friend Rose—someone I have known since we were 11 years old. This key lime flavor is totally her jam. Tart, sweet, creamy with a crunchy crust, these cheesecake bars are so packed with nutrients from the cashews, you would have no idea that you were eating something healthy.

Makes 12 bars

FOR THE CRUST

1 ½ c/390 g Gluten-Free Graham Crackers, crushed (page 49)

⅓ c/75 g vegan butter, melted

¼ c/50 g granulated sugar

2 Tbsp/28 g brown sugar, packed

FOR THE LIME FILLING

2 ½ c/640 g cashews, soaked for 1 to 2 hours

½ c/120 ml lime juice

¼ c/60 ml nondairy milk

¼ c/60 ml agave nectar or maple syrup

2 tsp/7.5 ml vanilla extract

Zest of 2 large limes

2 tsp/7.5 ml homemade green food coloring for more of a green hue (optional—page 161)

⅓ c/80 ml unrefined coconut oil, melted

ADD-ON

1 batch Coconut Whipped Cream (page 150)

Preheat oven to 350°F/180°C. Grease an 8 x 8-inch/20 x 20-cm pan.

Combine all of the ingredients for the crust until well mixed. Press into the pan and bake for 10 to 12 minutes. Allow to cool.

To make the filling, combine all the ingredients except for the coconut oil in a blender until completely smooth. If it is difficult to blend, add 1 tablespoon/ 15 ml of water at a time until the mix is able to blend properly. Try not to add too much, though—you want a thick filling.

Add the oil and blend until combined.

Pour over crust, cover with foil and chill in the fridge for several hours until firm. If you can allow it to set overnight, that is ideal. Top with homemade Coconut Whipped Cream for a decadent treat.

Chocolate Chip Blondie Ice Cream Sundaes

This is one of my favorite recipes in the book—it's outrageous how tasty these blondies are and how they don't even taste like they are missing the gluten, eggs and dairy! Reminiscent of a thick chocolate chip cookie bar, it seems like the right thing to do is coat them with a scoop of nondairy ice cream and drizzle with homemade Caramel Sauce (page 147).

Makes 9 squares

DRY

1 ½ c/248 g Cara's All-Purpose Blend (page 166)

1 tsp xanthan gum

1 tsp baking powder

½ tsp baking soda

½ tsp salt

¾ c/132 g nondairy chocolate chips

WET

½ c/112 g vegan butter

¼ c/60 ml nondairy milk

½ c/110 g packed brown sugar

½ c/100 g granulated sugar

3 tsp/9.5 g Ener-G Egg Replacer plus 6 Tbsp/90 ml warm water, mixed until frothy

1 tsp vanilla

ADD-ONS

1 pint of nondairy ice cream

1 batch Warmed-up Caramel Sauce (page 147)

Preheat oven to 350°F/180°C.

Whisk together the dry ingredients (except the chocolate chips) in a medium bowl.

In a medium saucepan, melt butter, milk and sugars, whisk on medium-low heat. Allow to cool for 5 to 10 minutes. Add the powdered egg replacer and vanilla into the sugar butter mix. Fold the dry ingredients into the butter mix. Fold in half the chocolate chips.

Line an 8 x 8-inch/20 x 20-cm pan with parchment paper or tinfoil, leaving the edges out so you can easily pull out once baked, and pour in the batter. Top with the remainder of the chocolate chips. Bake for 30 to 35 minutes or until slightly browned. The cookie base will continue to cook once you take it out of the oven, so make sure you don't let it sit longer in the oven or it will get too crispy on the inside.

Allow to cool just enough so you won't burn your fingers. Pull parchment paper out of the pan and allow the blondies to rest on the cooling rack until fully cooled.

Top with your favorite flavor of nondairy ice cream and my homemade Warmed-up Caramel Sauce.

Easy Vegan Fudge

This is a recipe favorite from my website Fork & Beans. I get e-mails and comments on a weekly basis about how easy it really is to make (See? The title isn't deceiving.) and how delicious it tastes. The fudge makes the perfect homemade gift but also tastes just as good when you eat it alone at home. Judge-free zone, friends.

Makes 25 small fudge squares

2 c/352 g nondairy chocolate chips

½ c/120 ml coconut cream (not coconut milk)

½ c/120 ml nondairy milk

½ tsp salt

1 c/120 g chopped walnuts

1 tsp vanilla extract

Line an 8 x 8-inch/20 x 20-cm square pan with wax paper.

In a heavy saucepan over low heat, melt nondairy chocolate chips or bar pieces with coconut cream, nondairy milk and salt until completely smooth. Remove from the heat. Stir in nuts if desired and vanilla. Place more chopped nuts on top if desired.

Chill 2 hours or until firm. Turn fudge onto cutting board, peel off paper and cut into squares. Store covered in fridge.

CARA'S TIP: Please note that this recipe calls for coconut cream, not coconut milk. There is a difference! Coconut cream contains 4 times less the amount of water than coconut milk, which allows for the fudge to set. It can be a little harder to find, depending on where you live, but thank God for the Internet!

chapter 3

DONUTS, MUFFINS, SCONES & BISCUITS

I have a real special spot in my heart for all things donuts, muffins, scones and biscuits. If I had the choice, I would make these sweet treats my breakfast every morning (if only my waistline would allow it). When I realized I had a dairy allergy, thoughts of delicious blueberry muffins danced in my head . . . and out the window. But once I got a handle on gluten-, egg- and dairy-free baking, I built up a recipe base that I am rather proud of. Thankfully, those muffins have found their way back into my life! Here is my homage to some of my favorite things like maple donuts and cranberry scones, oh my.

Brown Sugar Mini Donuts

I am donut obsessed. There, I said it. From when I was a little girl to now that I'm an adult, the simple suggestion of donuts prompts me to insatiably salivate until I get my hands on one. I'm not even kidding. It's so bad that I have reserved eating donuts to one time of the year: Christmas. It has now become my holiday tradition to get a donut on Christmas morning. Otherwise, I will eat them every week. Thankfully, these mini donuts are the perfect size to satiate any donut-frenzied sweet tooth. Plus, anything in mini form always increases the flavor. I mean, that's science, right?

Makes 12 mini donuts (or 6 regular-sized) from a donut pan

DRY
1 ½ c/248 g Cara's All-Purpose Blend (page 166)

½ c/73 g lightly packed brown sugar

2 tsp/7.5 g baking powder

½ tsp xanthan gum

¼ tsp salt

¼ tsp nutmeg

WET
½ c/120 ml nondairy milk plus 2 tsp/10 ml apple cider vinegar (or lemon juice)—soured for 10 minutes

1 ½ tsp/5 g Ener-G Egg Replacer plus 2 Tbsp/30 ml water—mixed until frothy

¼ c/60 ml vegetable oil, melted

½ tsp vanilla extract

Preheat oven to 350°F/180°C. Grease a donut pan of choice (either the 6 regular-sized or 12 mini-sized). I prefer the mini size because you can eat more.

In a medium bowl, whisk the dry ingredients together. Make a well in the center of the bowl and add all of the wet ingredients into that well. Stir with a wooden spoon until just incorporated.

Place batter into a large plastic baggie (I use this because I don't have a piping bag, but if you do, feel free to use it instead). Cut the corner of one side to use as an opening. Using one hand to firmly keep the dough flowing out of the hole, squirt the dough out in a circle in the pan. The more intact the dough comes out, the better the results in the end.

Bake 8 to 10 minutes. Allow to sit in the pan briefly until cool enough to handle, and then place each donut onto a cooling rack.

Frost or decorate with the variations on the next page.

> CARA'S TIP: If you want good old-fashioned iced donuts, I suggest dipping the tops in my Simple Donut Icing (page 157) and decorating them with homemade Rainbow sprinkles (page 163).

Maple-Frosted Donuts

These are hands-down my favorite version of donut to make on those cold mornings where you just want to snuggle up next to the fire with a cup of coffee. Oh who am I kidding? Any weather is the perfect time for maple and peanuts in a donut.

Brown Sugar Mini Donut recipe (page 65)
1 ½ c/180 g powdered sugar
¼ c/60 ml coconut oil, melted
2 Tbsp/30 ml maple syrup
½ tsp vanilla extract
2 Tbsp/30 ml hot water
½ c/66 g chopped peanuts

While the donuts are on the cooling rack, combine the powdered sugar into the melted oil and syrup in a shallow bowl. Add vanilla and water until thick but thin enough to stir with ease. Add more water if it is too thick or more powdered sugar if it is too thin.

With your fingers, gently dip the tops of the donuts into the icing and immediately top with chopped nuts. These take only a few minutes to set.

CARA'S TIP: When you are icing your donuts, do them one at a time so you can make sure to immediately top them with the chopped nuts. The icing will dry quickly and will not allow the nuts to set if you wait too long.

Chocolate-Frosted Donuts

Brown Sugar Mini Donut recipe (page 65)
1 c/176 g nondairy chocolate chips
1 Tbsp/14 g shortening or coconut oil

Place the nondairy chocolate into a microwave-safe bowl. On high, heat in 30-second intervals in the microwave, stirring at each stop. Repeat until just melted and smooth. Add the shortening into the bowl and mix until melted and smooth.

Gently place bottom of the donut into the bowl. Place a fork under the donut to hold it in place. With a spoon, drizzle the chocolate on top until the whole donut is covered with melted chocolate.

Place donut on a piece of wax paper to set. If you want it to set quickly, place in the fridge.

Pumpkin Spice Muffins

Don't be fooled. Pumpkin muffins aren't just for fall anymore. These are fit for every occasion: the muffins of all muffins—king of the baked goods! This is probably my opinion because I really believe that pumpkin is one of the greatest flavors known to man. Delicate, moist and full of flavor, I wouldn't be surprised if these become your go-to muffins.

Makes 12 muffins

FOR THE STREUSEL TOPPING
1 c/165 g Cara's All-Purpose blend (page 166)
½ c/110 g packed brown sugar
1 tsp cinnamon
Pinch of salt
5 Tbsp/70 g nondairy butter, cold and cut into small pieces
½ c/60 g walnuts, chopped (optional)

DRY
2 c/330 g Cara's All-Purpose blend (page 166)
¾ c/110 g lightly packed brown sugar
½ c/100 g granulated sugar
2 tsp/8.5 g baking soda
1 tsp baking powder
¾ tsp xanthan gum
1 ½ tsp cinnamon
¼ tsp nutmeg
¼ tsp ground cloves (optional)
½ tsp salt

WET
¾ c/184 g canned pumpkin purée (not the pie mix)
½ c/120 ml vegetable oil
¼ c/60 ml nondairy milk
¼ c/60 ml boiling water
1 Tbsp/15 ml apple cider vinegar (or lemon juice)

ADD-IN
½ c/60 g walnuts, chopped (optional)

Combine the first 4 ingredients for the streusel topping. Cut the butter into the flour mix until evenly combined. Toss in the chopped walnuts (you might have to get those beautiful fingers a bit dirty) and mix. Set aside.

Preheat oven to 350°F/180°C. Lightly grease or line a muffin pan.

In a large bowl, mix all of the dry ingredients together. In a medium bowl, thoroughly mix the wet ingredients together. Pour wet ingredients into the dry. With a wooden spoon mix until just combined. Fold in the walnuts (optional).

Pour batter into the muffin pan using a cupcake scoop. Garnish with streusel topping. Bake for 25 to 30 minutes until the knife comes out smooth when inserted. Allow to cool for a couple of minutes and transfer to a cooling rack.

Blueberry Pecan Muffins

Nothing beats the taste of muffins the moment they come out of the oven, does it? (Maybe chocolate chip cookies but we are talking muffins here.) Each muffin is bursting with the sweetness of blueberries, the crunch of pecans and a hint of cinnamon, giving you satisfaction in every bite. Just make sure that you allow your muffins to cool down a bit before you take your first bite. This will help them not crumble from the heat as well as save your mouth from getting burned. Consider this my public service announcement.

Makes 12 muffins

DRY

2 c/330 g Cara's All-Purpose Blend (page 166)
½ c/72.5 g lightly packed brown sugar
½ c/100 g granulated sugar
2 tsp/7.5 g baking powder
1 tsp baking soda
1 tsp xanthan gum
½ tsp salt

WET

½ c/120 ml oil
1 c/240 g applesauce
½ c/120 ml warmed nondairy milk
1 Tbsp/15 ml apple cider vinegar (or lemon juice)

ADD-INS

1 c/140 g frozen blueberries
½ c/60 g toasted pecans, chopped

Preheat oven to 350°F/180°C. Lightly grease or line a muffin pan.

In a medium bowl, combine the dry ingredients. In a small bowl, combine the wet ingredients. Whisk until combined.

Make a well in the dry mix and pour the wet mix in. Stir with a wooden spoon until just combined. Fold in the blueberries and pecans. Pour batter into the muffin pan.

Bake for 22 to 25 minutes or until the muffins are firm on the top and spring back when touched. Immediately transfer to a cooling rack.

> **CARA'S TIP:** Spruce up these muffins with a streusel topping to give that added oomph.
>
> 1 c/165 g Cara's All-Purpose Blend (page 166)
> ½ c/110 g packed brown sugar
> 1 tsp cinnamon, pinch of salt
> 5 Tbsp/70 g nondairy butter, cold and cut into small pieces
>
> Whisk everything together except for the butter until well combined. Cut in the butter until it resembles small lumps. Sprinkle over the batter in the muffin pan before baking.

Death by Chocolate Muffins

What is the secret of that extra boost in these chocolate chip muffins, you ask? Why, it's pumpkin purée of course. Pumpkin can be the winning key ingredient in gluten-free and vegan baking. Not only does it enable the rise and binding of the baked good, but it also creates a super-moist bite. If you can find a way to incorporate pumpkin purée into every recipe, I say do it!

Makes 12 muffins

DRY

2 c/330 g Cara's All-Purpose Blend (page 166)

¼ c/22 g cocoa powder

½ c/72.5 g lightly packed brown sugar

½ c/100 g granulated sugar

2 tsp/7.5 g baking powder

1 tsp baking soda

1 tsp xanthan gum

½ tsp salt

WET

¾ c/184 g canned pumpkin purée (not the pie mix)

½ c/120 ml oil

¼ c/60 ml nondairy milk

¼ c/60 ml hot water

1 Tbsp/15 ml apple cider vinegar (or lemon juice)

ADD-IN

1 c/176 g nondairy chocolate chips

Preheat oven to 350°F/180°C. Lightly grease or line a muffin pan.

In a large bowl, mix all of the dry ingredients together. In a medium bowl, thoroughly mix the wet ingredients together. Pour wet ingredients into the dry. With a wooden spoon mix until just combined. Fold in the nondairy chocolate chips.

Pour batter into a muffin pan using a cupcake scoop. Bake for 25 to 30 minutes until knife comes out smooth when inserted. Allow to cool for a couple of minutes and transfer to a cooling rack.

CARA'S TIP: Allergic to pumpkin? A simple solution: Replace the purée with applesauce.

Banana Buckwheat Muffins

Bananas are great egg substitutes, so the ripe bananas in this recipe automatically provide a super-moist, tender bite in each muffin. The buckwheat flour adds a beautiful brown color and provides for a nutritiously dense breakfast. I fed these to my sweet friend Fanny, who is neither gluten-free nor vegan to see what she thought. She gave these muffins her seal of approval. I trust Fanny. So should you.

Makes 12 muffins

DRY

1 ½ c/248 g Cara's All-Purpose Blend (page 166)

½ c/60 g buckwheat flour

¾ c/108 g lightly packed brown sugar

½ c/100 g sugar

2 tsp/7.5 g baking powder

1 tsp baking soda

¾ tsp xanthan gum

1 tsp cinnamon

½ tsp nutmeg

½ tsp salt

WET

1 c/225 g mashed bananas (approximately 3 medium bananas)

½ c/120 ml oil

¼ c/60 ml nondairy milk

¼ c/60 ml hot water

1 Tbsp/15 ml apple cider vinegar (or lemon juice)

½ tsp vanilla extract

ADD-IN

½ c/60 g walnuts or pecans, chopped (optional)

Preheat oven to 350°F/180°C. Lightly grease or line a muffin pan.

In a medium bowl, mix all of the dry ingredients together. In a large bowl, thoroughly mash the bananas with an electric mixer. Add the remainder of the wet ingredients together and blend until mixed. Beat in the dry mix until just combined. Fold in the walnuts. Pour batter into the muffin pan and bake for 22 to 25 minutes or until a toothpick comes out clean when inserted.

Allow to cool briefly, and then transfer to cooling rack.

Good Morning Muffins

Forget Pop-Tarts, these muffins are the new, perfect on-the-go breakfast for those who are in a hurry. Grab one for the road when you are pressed for time and eat on the way to wherever your final destination is. These muffins are hearty and chockfull of nuts and seeds—a nutrient-dense food that will satisfy your tummy and brain.

Makes 12 muffins

DRY

2 c/330 g Cara's All-Purpose Blend (page 166)

½ c/72.5 g lightly packed brown sugar

¼ c/50 g granulated sugar

¼ c/30 g buckwheat flour

2 tsp/7.5 g baking powder

1 tsp baking soda

½ tsp salt

1 Tbsp/7 g flaxseed meal

1 tsp xanthan gum

1 tsp cinnamon

¼ tsp nutmeg

WET

1 c/240 ml nondairy milk

⅓ c/80 ml vegetable oil

1 Tbsp/15 ml apple cider vinegar (or lemon juice)

ADD-INS

¼ c/35 g sunflower seeds, raw

¼ c/30 g walnuts, chopped

¼ c/30 g toasted pecans, chopped

Gluten-free rolled oats for topping

Preheat oven to 350°F/180°C. Lightly grease or line a muffin pan.

In a large bowl, whisk together all of the dry ingredients. In a medium bowl, combine the wet ingredients. Make a well in the middle of the dry ingredients and pour the milk mixture in. Stir with a wooden spoon. Fold in the add-ins. Pour the batter into the muffin pan. Top wiht the gluten-free rolled oats.

Bake for 22 to 25 minutes or until a knife comes out clean when inserted. Allow to cool slightly before removing from the muffin tins. Cool on a wire rack.

Cinnamon Coffee Cake Muffins

Maybe they are not the healthiest option for breakfast, but these coffee cake muffins pair perfectly with, well, a cup of coffee (too obvious?) when you need to satisfy that sweet tooth midday. I like to make a half batch of these muffins whenever a special friend comes over and we need a tasty treat to snack on when exchanging some serious gossip.

Makes 10 muffins

DRY
2 c/330 g Cara's All-Purpose Blend (page 166)

½ c/72.5 g unpacked brown sugar

¼ c/50 g granulated sugar

2 tsp/7.5 g baking powder

1 tsp baking soda

½ tsp salt

1 Tbsp/7 g flaxseed meal

1 tsp xanthan gum

1 tsp cinnamon

¼ tsp nutmeg

WET
¾ c/180 ml nondairy milk

⅓ c/80 ml oil

1 Tbsp/15 ml apple cider vinegar (or lemon juice)

FOR THE STREUSEL TOPPING
1 c/165 g Cara's All-Purpose Flour Blend (page 166)

⅓ c/73 g brown sugar, lightly packed

2 tsp/5 g cinnamon

3 Tbsp/42 g vegan butter

ADD-ON
½ batch Royal Icing (page 158)

Preheat oven to 350°F/180°C. Lightly grease or line a muffin pan.

In a large bowl, whisk together all of the dry ingredients. In a medium bowl, combine the wet ingredients. Make a well in the middle of the dry ingredients and pour the milk mixture in. Stir with a wooden spoon. Pour the batter into the muffin pan. Combine the ingredients for the streusel topping and sprinkle it evenly on the batter.

Bake for 22 to 25 minutes or until a knife comes out clean when inserted. Allow to cool slightly before removing from the muffin tins. Cool on a wire rack. Drizzle with half a batch of Royal Icing.

CARA'S TIP: If you have spots in your muffin tin that are not filled before going into the oven, place some water halfway inside the individual spots. By doing this, you ensure that all of your muffins will be baked evenly.

Upside-Down Sticky Pecan Biscuits

These upside-down biscuits are a real showstopper. Not only are they gorgeous to the eye, but they are also bursting with flavor. Made from a simple biscuit base, they turn into a cinnamon-rolled treat topped with maple syrup and pecans. I cannot say enough good things about these; just go now and start baking, okay?

Makes 12 pecan biscuits

FOR THE PECAN SUGAR TOPPING
3 Tbsp/42 g vegan butter
½ c/72.5 g brown sugar
2 Tbsp/30 ml maple syrup
1 c/120 g chopped toasted pecans

FOR THE FILLING
2 Tbsp/28 g vegan butter, melted
¼ c/36 g brown sugar
2 Tbsp/26 g granulated sugar

DRY
2 c/330 g Cara's Special Blend (page 166)
¼ c/30 g chopped pecans
1 tsp xanthan gum
1 tsp baking soda
½ tsp baking powder
Pinch of salt

WET
2 Tbsp/28 g vegan butter
1 Tbsp/14 g non-hydrogenated shortening
½ c/120 ml nondairy milk
¼ c/60 ml canned coconut milk, full fat
1 Tbsp/15 ml apple cider vinegar (or lemon juice)

In a small saucepan, melt the vegan butter and brown sugar until dissolved. Add the syrup and pecans and allow to heat through for 5 minutes. Do not allow it to burn. Heavily grease (include the top too) a muffin pan and evenly distribute about 2 teaspoons/5 g of the pecan sugar topping into every slot.

Preheat oven to 375°F/190°C. Line a baking sheet with parchment paper.

In a small bowl, combine all of the ingredients for the filling and set aside. In a large mixing bowl, combine the dry ingredients. Cut in the vegan butter and shortening until evenly distributed and small crumbles appear. Mix in the remainder of the wet ingredients and stir with a wooden spoon until everything is combined and dough has been formed. If the dough is still too sticky at this point, add 1 tablespoon/8 g of gluten-free flour at a time until it is no longer sticky.

Place half the dough on top of a piece of parchment paper and very lightly coat with gluten-free flour. With your hands, form your dough into a large rectangle 9 x 12 inches/22.5 x 30 cm and spread the filling over it. Sprinkle half of the sugar mixture over the batter. Roll the dough from the length side over and cut into six 2-inch/5-cm pieces. Place each roll into the muffin tin and lightly spread and pat each piece down to ensure they fit into the entire space. Repeat with the other half of the dough.

Place the muffin pan on the parchment paper–lined baking sheet (the sugar will bubble over and this will protect your oven) and bake for 18 to 20 minutes.

When removing the biscuits from the muffin pan, the topping won't necessarily come out with it, so just place the biscuit rolls onto a wire rack and immediately spoon the mixture back onto the tops. Allow the sugar to set for 5 minutes before serving.

CARA'S TIP: Don't worry if the sugar from the bottom rises over on top of your muffin pan. It will easily remove. Once you remove the biscuits from the pan and spoon the sugar back on top, wipe off the melted sugar and immediately place in water. Careful, it will be hot.

Shortcake Biscuits

These shortcakes sure beat the store-bought packages you find at your local market around summertime. It's a simple biscuit recipe with a hint of sweetness that once cracked open, pairs perfectly with fresh berries and homemade nondairy whipped cream for a shortcake biscuit sandwich.

Makes 8 shortcakes

DRY

1 ½ c/248 g Cara's Special Blend (page 166)

¼ c/50 g granulated sugar

2 ½ tsp/9.5 g baking powder

1 tsp xanthan gum

Pinch of salt

WET

1 Tbsp/14 g vegan butter, chilled and cubed

2 Tbsp/28 g non-hydrogenated shortening, chilled and cubed

⅓ c/80 ml light coconut milk, canned (or nondairy milk of choice)

ADD-ONS

Fresh berries

1 batch Strawberry Whipped Cream (page 152)

Preheat oven to 400°F/200°C. Line a baking sheet with parchment paper.

In a large mixing bowl, combine the dry ingredients. Cut in the vegan butter and shortening until evenly distributed. Mix in the coconut milk (or nondairy milk of choice). Knead together until the dough is slightly sticky.

On a piece of parchment paper lightly coated with gluten-free flour, place the dough and gently spread out into a circle that is 1 ½ inches/3.75 cm thick. Cut into circles with 2-inch/5-cm biscuit cutters and place on the baking sheet.

Bake for 10 to 13 minutes or until brown. Allow to cool on a wire rack and cut biscuit in half. Place fresh berries on top and dollop with my homemade Strawberry Whipped Cream for the perfect shortcake.

Chocolate Indulgence Biscuits

Biscuits are no longer for the savory breakfast lover, oh no! The only kind of gravy I want smothered on these bad boys is the kind that consists of Homemade Chocolate Sauce (page 149), chocolate chips, cocoa powder and topped off with some more homemade Chocolate Dream Whipped Cream (page 152). You get the point—these are a decadent chocolaty good dessert.

MAKES 8 BISCUITS

DRY

1 ½ c/248 g Cara's All-Purpose Blend (page 166)

¼ c/22 g cocoa powder

¼ c/55 g brown sugar, packed

1 tsp xanthan gum

1 tsp baking powder

½ tsp baking soda

¼ tsp salt

WET

2 Tbsp/28 g vegan butter, chilled and cubed

1 Tbsp/14 g non-hydrogenated shortening, chilled and cubed

½ c/120 ml canned light coconut milk (or nondairy milk of choice)

1 Tbsp/15 ml apple cider vinegar (or lemon juice)

ADD-IN

½ c/90 g nondairy chocolate chips

Preheat oven to 400°F/200°C. Line a baking sheet with parchment paper.

In a large mixing bowl, combine the dry ingredients. Cut in the vegan butter and shortening until evenly distributed. Mix in the nondairy milk and vinegar. Knead together with your hands just until the flour gets incorporated and your dough becomes slightly sticky. It should be easy to work with—if not, add 1 tablespoon/10 g of gluten-free flour at a time until it is.

Place the dough on top of a piece of parchment paper and very lightly coat with cocoa powder to make the dough easy to work with. With your hands, form your dough into a large circle that is 1 ½ inch/3.75 cm thick. Cut into circles with 2-inch/5-cm biscuit cutters and place on the baking sheet. You might need to pat dough pieces back together to get the full 8 circle cutouts.

Bake for 12 to 15 minutes or until brown. Allow to cool on a wire rack and cut biscuits in half.

CRACKED PEPPER AND HERB DROP BISCUITS

Need an easy-to-whip-up bread for dinner? Drop biscuits are the easiest and quickest way to ensure that your homemade soup is no longer lonely for dinner. Instead of using a biscuit cutter, all you have to do is drop the dough onto the baking sheet from the spoon (hence its name). Easy, right? Don't like the add-ins listed? Add whatever floats your boat. That is, if you have a boat.

MAKES 12 DROP BISCUITS

DRY

1 ½ c/190 g Cara's Special Blend (page 166)

1 tsp xanthan gum

2 ½ tsp/9.5 g baking powder

1 tsp fresh rosemary, minced

1 tsp fresh thyme, minced

1 tsp fresh parsley, minced

1 tsp fresh ground pepper

½ tsp salt

WET

1 Tbsp/14 g vegan butter, chilled and cubed

2 Tbsp/28 g non-hydrogenated shortening, chilled and cubed

⅓ c/75 ml light coconut milk, canned

Preheat oven to 400°/200°C. Line a baking sheet with parchment paper.

In a large mixing bowl, combine flour, xanthan gum, baking powder, dried herbs, pepper and salt. Cut butter and shortening into the dry ingredients until fully incorporated. Add the coconut milk and mix.

Drop by the spoonful, 3 inches/7.5 cm in size, onto the baking sheet. Bake for 10 to 13 minutes or until brown. Allow to cool slightly.

WILD BLUEBERRY SCONES

Isn't it funny how food reminds you of certain people? Blueberry scones will forever be associated with one of my best friends, Brooke. She was the first person I met in college and though it took a few years for us to reunite, once we did we were inseparable. Both of us had wild, curly blonde hair, we wore flip flops every day and dined on blueberry scones over a good cup of coffee while we talked about God. We were like two peas in a pod. We now live on opposite sides of California, but just the mere thought of a blueberry scone brings me back to those college days and missing Brooke and those Italian curls.

MAKES 6 SCONES

2 c/330 g Cara's All-Purpose Blend (page 166)

¾ tsp xanthan gum

1 Tbsp/16 g baking powder

½ tsp salt

¼ c/50 g granulated sugar

5 Tbsp/70 g vegan butter, cold and cubed

1 c/240 ml light coconut milk, canned

2 tsp/6.5 g lemon zest

1 c/140 g frozen wild blueberries

Coarse sugar for garnish

FOR THE "EGG" WASH

1 Tbsp/15 ml water

2 tsp/6.5 g cornstarch

Preheat oven to 425°F/220°C. Line a baking sheet with a piece of parchment paper.

Whisk the flour, xanthan, baking powder, salt and sugar together. With a pastry blender, add the butter into the flour mix until crumbly. Stir in coconut milk. Before you completely combine the dough together, add the lemon zest and blueberries. Mix until flour is completely combined.

Gently pat dough into a circle (approximately 8-inch/20-cm diameter). Slice the scones into 6 pieces. Sprinkle with coarse sugar and place on a greased baking sheet and coat a thin layer of the "egg" wash by whisking the water and cornstarch together, and then gliding onto the dough with a brush. Bake 15 to 20 minutes or until lightly browned. Allow to cool on a baking rack for 10 minutes.

CRANBERRY ORANGE SCONES

My very talented friend Celine of Have Cake Will Travel gave me the title of Scone Queen. Coming from someone who knows her baked goods, this is one of the nicest compliments anyone could give me. But don't take her word for it—test it out for yourself and see what all the gossip is about!

MAKES 6 SCONES

DRY
2 c/330 g Cara's All-Purpose Blend (page 166)
¾ tsp xanthan gum
1 Tbsp/16 g baking powder
½ tsp salt
¼ c/50 g granulated sugar

WET
5 Tbsp/70 g vegan butter, cold and cubed
1 c/240 ml light coconut milk, canned
2 tsp/4 g orange zest
1 c/120 g dried cranberries

FOR "EGG" WASH
1 Tbsp/15 ml water
2 tsp/6.5 g cornstarch

FOR SUGAR GLAZE
1 c/120 g powdered sugar
1–2 tsp/5-10 ml orange juice
1 tsp orange zest

Preheat oven to 425°F/220°C.

Whisk the flour, xanthan, baking powder, salt and sugar together. With a pastry blender, add the butter into the flour mix until crumbly. Stir in milk. Before you completely combine the dough together, add the zest and cranberries. Mix until flour is completely combined.

Gently pat dough into a circle (approximately 8-inch/20-cm diameter). Slice the scones into 6 pieces and place on a greased baking sheet and coat a thin layer of the "egg" wash by whisking the water and cornstarch together, and then gliding onto the dough with a brush. Bake 15 to 20 minutes or until light browned. Allow to cool on a baking rack for 10 minutes. Coat the tops of the scones with the sugar glaze.

TO MAKE THE GLAZE
Combine all ingredients to make a paste thick enough to stir but not too runny.

Maple Nut Scones

Back in my Starbucks days, I used to eat maple nut scones on a daily basis. No really, I'm not just saying this to be silly—I used to have a serious problem with eating pastries at work, which inevitably left me with a bloated and upset belly. Needless to say, scones were my weakness. Thankfully this recipe is gentle on my belly, and I no longer have any issues with eating them. Pass me the scones!

Makes 6 scones

DRY
2 c/250 g Cara's Special Blend (page 166)
¾ tsp xanthan gum
1 Tbsp/16 g baking powder
½ tsp salt

WET
5 Tbsp/70 g vegan butter, cold and cubed
¾ c/180 ml light coconut milk, canned
¼ c/80 ml maple syrup
¼ tsp maple extract

FOR THE "EGG" WASH
1 Tbsp/15 ml water
2 tsp/6.5 g cornstarch

FOR MAPLE SYRUP GLAZE
1 ½ c/180 g powdered sugar
1 Tbsp/15 ml maple syrup
1 Tbsp/15 ml hot water
2 tsp /10 ml melted coconut oil
½ tsp maple extract

½ c/60 g toasted pecans, chopped

Preheat oven to 425°F/220°C. Line a baking sheet with a piece of parchment paper.

Whisk the flour, xanthan, baking powder and salt together. With a pastry blender, add the butter into the flour mix until crumbly. Stir in milk, syrup and maple extract and mix until completely combined.

Gently pat dough into a circle (approximately 8-inch/20-cm diameter). Slice the scones into 6 pieces and place on a greased baking sheet and coat a thin layer of the "egg" wash by whisking the water and cornstarch together, and then gliding it onto the dough with a brush. Bake 15 to 20 minutes or until lightly browned. Allow to cool on a baking rack for 10 minutes. Coat the tops of the scones with the maple syrup glaze and top with chopped pecans.

To make the glaze
Combine all ingredients to make a paste thick enough to stir but not so thin it will run off the spoon quickly.

CARA'S TIP: If you do not have maple extract, simply omit it. The taste from the maple syrup will be sufficient to flavor the scones. The extract is for the serious maple syrup lovers. Also, if you do not want to use coconut milk, use a nondairy milk of choice.

Yeast-Free Cinnamon Buns

I get a lot of feedback about people's experiences with yeast and how frustrating it can be. Either they are unable to properly proof it, or for some reason it falls flat throughout the duration of baking. I would hate for those people to have to skip out on one of the greatest foods ever, cinnamon rolls, just because of yeast, so I created a recipe that is made from biscuit-like dough. Look at that! We all win and get to eat cinnamon rolls.

Makes 8 cinnamon buns

DRY

3 c/495 g Cara's All-Purpose Blend (page 166)

2 tsp/7.5 g baking powder

½ tsp baking soda

1 ½ tsp /5 g xanthan gum

½ tsp salt

WET

1 ½ c/360 ml nondairy milk

1 Tbsp/15 ml apple cider vinegar (or lemon juice)

6 Tbsp/84 g vegan butter, melted (divide into 3)

FOR THE CINNAMON SUGAR FILLING

1 c/220 g brown sugar, packed

2 Tbsp/28 g vegan butter or coconut oil, melted

2 tsp/5 g cinnamon

⅛ tsp ground cloves

FOR THE ICING

1 ½ c/180 g powdered sugar

¼ c/60 ml melted coconut oil

½ tsp vanilla extract

2 Tbsp/30 ml hot water

Preheat oven to 425°F/220°C. Grease an 8-inch/20-cm round glass or tin pie pan.

Combine 2 ½ cups/413 g of the flour (set ½ cup/83 g to the side) and the remainder of the dry ingredients until well blended. In a small bowl, whisk together the nondairy milk, vinegar and 2 tablespoons/28 g of the melted butter. Add the liquid ingredients into the large bowl with the flour mixture and stir with a wooden spoon until the liquid is absorbed. The dough will look ugly at this point.

Line the counter with a piece of parchment paper and coat with ¼ cup/41 g of the reserved flour mix. Transfer the dough onto the floured counter and begin kneading until the flour is incorporated. Add the remainder of the flour reserve until the dough becomes less sticky and easier to work with.

To make the filling

Combine all the ingredients in a bowl until it's the texture of wet sand and set aside.

With your hands, shape the dough gently into a 9 x 13-inch/22.5 x 32.5-cm rectangle. Spread 2 tablespoons/28 g of the melted butter and evenly sprinkle the cinnamon-sugar filling onto the dough. Using the parchment paper to guide you, roll the dough from the length side over. If your dough breaks apart at the seams, just use your hands and pat the dough to correct the problem. Slice the roll into 8 even pieces.

Place each piece into the greased pan. Brush the top of the rolls with the remaining 2 tablespoons/28 g of the melted vegan butter. Bake for 18 to 22 minutes or until golden brown. Allow to cool slightly for about 5 minutes before coating with the icing.

To make the icing

Combine sugar into melted oil. Add vanilla and water until thick but thin enough to stir with ease. Add more water if too thick or more powdered sugar if too thin.

chapter 4

CUPCAKES & CAKES

Make that special occasion even more special by baking a cake or cupcake from this chapter for your loved ones. Full of ideas to celebrate those moments in your life when a sweet treat really says it all, here is a wonderful selection for you to choose from. Looking for a chocolate cupcake coated with a creamy peanut butter frosting that you can sink your teeth into? You came to the right place, friends. What about a cake stacked high with a coconut walnut icing? It's called utter perfection. You can even make me one of the following recipes for my birthday. It's in November. I will send you my address.

GINGERBREAD CUPCAKES

Is it just me or does the decorative mini gingerbread man make this recipe all the more delectable? It's just me, isn't it? How about if I told you that about halfway through the baking time of these cupcakes your home will smell like ginger, nutmeg and molasses? I knew that would capture your attention.

Makes 12 cupcakes

DRY
2 c/330 g Cara's All-Purpose Blend (page 166)
½ c/73 g lightly packed brown sugar
2 tsp/7.5 g baking powder
1 tsp baking soda
1 ½ tsp/4 g ground ginger
1 tsp cinnamon
¼ tsp nutmeg
½ tsp salt

WET
1 c/245 g pumpkin, canned (not the pie mix)
½ c/120 ml oil
½ c/120 ml nondairy milk
½ c/176 g molasses

ADD-ONS
1 batch Cinnamon-Spiced Buttercream Frosting (page 153)
Ginger Wafer Thins (page 44)

Preheat oven to 350°F/180°C. Lightly grease or line a muffin pan.

In a large bowl, mix all of the dry ingredients together. Separately, in a medium bowl, thoroughly mix the wet ingredients together.

Pour wet ingredients into the dry. With a wooden spoon, mix until the batter is just combined. Pour batter into the cupcake pan using a cupcake scoop. Bake for 15 to 18 minutes until knife comes out smooth when inserted.

Allow to cool for a couple of minutes, and then transfer to a cooling rack. Frost each cupcake with Cinnamon-Spiced Buttercream Frosting, and for an added touch, place a Ginger Wafer Thin on top.

Strawberry Shortcake Cupcakes

Light, fresh and reminiscent of a summer berry shortcake, these cupcakes are sure to bring you back to the days when you were obsessed with Strawberry Shortcake dolls and your bed was covered in Strawberry Shortcake bed sheets. What? I grew up in the eighties, can you blame me? I can still smell those scratch n' sniff stickers.

Makes 12 cupcakes

DRY

2 ½ c/413 g Cara's All-Purpose Blend (page 166)

1 c/200 g granulated sugar

1 tsp baking powder

1 tsp baking soda

½ tsp salt

WET

1 ½ c/398 ml full-fat coconut milk, canned

6 Tbsp/15 g applesauce

¼ c/60 ml hot water

1 Tbsp/15 ml apple cider vinegar (or lemon juice)

2 tsp/6.5 g lemon zest

1 tsp vanilla extract

ADD-ONS

1 c/150 g fresh strawberries, stems removed and finely chopped

1 batch Strawberry Whipped Cream (page 152)

Preheat oven to 350°F/180°C. Grease or line a muffin pan.

In a large bowl, whisk together the dry ingredients. In a medium bowl, combine the wet together until well mixed. Pour the wet ingredients into the dry ingredients and stir with a wooden spoon until just combined. Fold in the strawberries.

Pour into the muffin pan and bake for 18 to 20 minutes. Remove cupcakes from pan and allow to cool on the cooling rack. Once cooled, top with my homemade Strawberry Whipped Cream and garnish with sliced fresh strawberries.

PEANUT BUTTER CHOCOLATE CUPCAKES

If ever I am presented with the dilemma as to which cupcake is my favorite flavor combination, hands-down it has to be peanut butter and chocolate. I am definitely my father's daughter (a man who for his birthday demands us to bring him chocolate peanut butter ice cream for celebration—he will accept nothing less!). I love the slight saltiness of the peanut butter paired with the sweet chocolate. Sheer perfection.

MAKES 12 CUPCAKES

DRY

1 ½ c/248 g Cara's All-Purpose Blend (page 166)

¾ c/66 g cocoa powder

½ c/73 g lightly packed brown sugar

½ c/100 g granulated sugar

2 tsp/7.5 g baking powder

½ tsp baking soda

1 tsp xanthan gum

½ tsp salt

WET

1 c/240 ml nondairy milk

½ c/120 ml hot water

½ c/120 ml vegetable oil

2 Tbsp/14 g flaxseed meal plus 6 Tbsp/90 ml water—thickened for 5 minutes

1 Tbsp/15 ml apple cider vinegar (or lemon juice)

½ tsp vanilla extract

ADD-ONS

1 batch Nutter Butter Frosting (page 156)

½ c/88 g nondairy chocolate, melted

Preheat oven to 350°F/180°C. Grease or line a muffin pan.

In a large bowl, whisk together the dry ingredients. In a medium bowl, combine the wet together until well mixed. Pour the wet ingredients into the dry ingredients and stir with a wooden spoon until just combined.

Pour into the muffin pan and bake for 17 to 20 minutes. Remove cupcakes from pan and allow to cool on a wire rack. Frost with Nutter Butter Frosting and drizzle with melted nondairy chocolate. Feeling even crazier? Top with a chocolate-covered peanut.

Mexican Hot Chocolate Cupcakes

Visiting my sister at college down in San Diego, California, was one of my favorite things to do when I was in high school. I remember when she took me to a coffee shop—when coffee shops were just becoming cool—(Does that give away my age?) she made me try something called Mexican hot chocolate. I had dreams about the stuff months after! Creamy, chocolaty and spicy—the flavor combinations blew my mind. Perfect with that kick in the back of your throat, these cupcakes embody that very first cup of spiced cocoa.

Makes 12 cupcakes

DRY
1 ½ c/248 g Cara's All-Purpose Blend (page 166)

¾ c/66 g cocoa powder

½ c/73 g lightly packed brown sugar

½ c/100 g granulated sugar

2 tsp/7.5 g baking powder

½ tsp baking soda

1 tsp xanthan gum

1 tsp cinnamon

½ tsp nutmeg

¼ tsp cayenne pepper

½ tsp salt

WET
1 c/240 ml nondairy milk

½ c/120 ml hot water

½ c/120 ml vegetable oil

2 Tbsp/14 g flaxseed meal plus 6 Tbsp/90 ml water—thickened for 5 minutes

1 Tbsp/15 ml apple cider vinegar (or lemon juice)

½ tsp vanilla extract

½ c/88 g nondairy chocolate chips

ADD-ONS
1 batch Coconut Whipped Cream (page 150)

Cayenne pepper

Preheat oven to 350°F/180°C. Grease or line a muffin pan.

In a large bowl, whisk together the dry ingredients. In a medium bowl, combine the wet together until well mixed. Pour the wet ingredients into the dry ingredients, and then stir with a wooden spoon until just combined. Fold in the chocolate chips.

Pour into the muffin pan and bake for 17 to 20 minutes. Remove cupcakes from pan to cool on a wire rack. Frost with Coconut Whipped Cream and a sprinkle of cayenne pepper to make it a truly authentic experience, or try my Cinnamon-Spiced Buttercream Frosting (page 153) if you don't want to wait for the cream to set.

Pumpkin Cupcakes

A cupcake for the season, the flavor of pumpkin brings out the festive cheer within.
Tinted with cinnamon and nutmeg, the Cream Cheese Frosting brings out each spice.
Oh man, my mouth is watering just thinking about these.

Makes 12 cupcakes

DRY

2 ½ c/413 g Cara's All-Purpose Blend
(page 166)

1 ¼ c/250 g granulated sugar

2 tsp/8.5 g baking soda

1 tsp baking powder

1 tsp xanthan gum

1 tsp cinnamon

½ tsp salt

¼ tsp nutmeg

WET

¾ c/184 g canned pumpkin purée
(not the pie mix)

½ c/120 ml vegetable oil

½ c/120 ml hot water

½ c/120 ml nondairy milk

1 Tbsp/15 ml apple cider vinegar
(or lemon juice)

ADD-ONS

1 batch Cream Cheese Frosting
(page 155)

½ tsp cinnamon

¼ tsp nutmeg

Preheat oven to 350°F/180°C. Lightly grease or line a muffin pan.

In a large bowl, mix all of the dry ingredients together. Separately, in a medium bowl, thoroughly mix the wet ingredients together.

Pour wet ingredients into the dry. With a wooden spoon, mix until the batter is just combined. Pour batter into the cupcake pan using a cupcake scoop. Bake for 17 to 20 minutes until knife comes out smooth when inserted.

Allow to cool for a couple of minutes, and then transfer to a cooling rack. For the spiced cream cheese frosting, use the Cream Cheese Frosting base. Add ½ teaspoon cinnamon and ¼ teaspoon nutmeg at the end with the electric mixer.

Lemonade Stand Cupcakes

Consider this recipe my way of honoring that entrepreneur in all of us who had a homemade lemonade stand as a kid. Lemon on lemon, those lips are sure to pucker with delight.

Makes 12 cupcakes

DRY

2 ½ c/413 g Cara's All-Purpose Blend (page 166)

1 c/200 g granulated sugar

2 tsp/7.5 g baking powder

1 tsp baking soda

½ tsp salt

WET

1 ½ c/398 ml full-fat coconut milk, canned

6 Tbsp/90 g applesauce

¼ c/60 ml hot water

1 Tbsp/15 ml apple cider vinegar (or lemon juice)

1 Tbsp/13 g lemon zest

1 tsp vanilla extract

ADD-ONS

1 batch Lemon Drop Frosting (page 155)

1 batch Sugar Glitter (page 161)

Preheat oven to 350°F/180°C. Grease or line a muffin pan.

In a large bowl, whisk together the dry ingredients. In a medium bowl, combine the wet until well mixed. Pour the wet ingredients into the dry ingredients, and then stir with a wooden spoon until just combined.

Pour into the muffin pan and bake for 17 to 20 minutes. Remove cupcakes from pan and allow to cool on a wire rack. Once cooled, top with Lemon Drop Frosting and garnish with a striped straw and yellow-colored Sugar Glitter.

THE BLACKOUT CAKE

I'm conflicted why I named this the Blackout Cake—it's either because this cake is tall, completely dark and delicious or because after one slice the sugar overload will surely cause a blackout. I guess I will leave the decision up to your choosing.

MAKES 8 SLICES

DRY

2 ½ c/413 g Cara's All-Purpose Blend (page 166)

¾ c/66 g cocoa powder

½ c/73 g lightly packed brown sugar

½ c/100 g granulated sugar

2 tsp/7.5 g baking powder

1 tsp baking soda

1 tsp xanthan gum

½ tsp salt

WET

1 c/240 ml light coconut milk, canned

½ c/120 ml hot water

½ c/120 ml vegetable oil

½ c/122 g applesauce

½ tsp vanilla extract

ADD-ONS

1 batch Fluffy Dark Chocolate Frosting (page 153)

Nondairy chocolate chips

Preheat oven to 350°F/180°C. Grease two 8–inch/20–cm round pans.

In a large bowl, whisk together the dry ingredients. In a medium bowl, combine the wet until well mixed. Pour the wet ingredients into the dry ingredients and stir with a wooden spoon until just combined.

Pour into the round pans and bake for 25 to 30 minutes until a knife comes out smooth when inserted. Cool on a wire rack inside the pans for 5 minutes, and then remove to cool fully.

Once completely cooled, gently even out the top of one of the cakes to make it level. Spread Fluffy Dark Chocolate Frosting on top of it, and then layer on the second cake. Frost the entire cake with Fluffy Dark Chocolate Frosting. Top with nondairy chocolate chips for those special occasions.

German Chocolate Cake

Ooey gooey, decadent chocolate with coconut and walnuts—holy moly, my mouth is watering just thinking about this cake. If you make this and do it as a four-layered cake smothered with the delicious coconut frosting, I say call me up—I'm coming over for a slice!

Makes 8 slices

DRY

2 ½ c/413 g Cara's All-Purpose Blend (page 166)

¾ c/22 g cocoa powder

½ c/73 g lightly packed brown sugar

½ c/100 g granulated sugar

2 tsp/7.5 g baking powder

1 tsp baking soda

1 tsp xanthan gum

½ tsp salt

WET

1 c/240 ml light coconut milk, canned

½ c/120 ml hot water

½ c/120 ml vegetable oil

2 Tbsp/14 g flaxseed meal plus 6 Tbsp/90 ml water—thickened for 5 minutes

1 Tbsp/15 ml apple cider vinegar (or lemon juice)

½ tsp vanilla extract

ADD-ONS

1 batch Coconut Walnut Icing (page 157)

Chopped walnuts (optional)

Preheat oven to 350°F/180°C. Grease two 8-inch/20-cm round pans.

In a large bowl, whisk together the dry ingredients. In a medium bowl, combine the wet until well mixed. Pour the wet ingredients into the dry ingredients and stir with a wooden spoon until just combined.

Pour into the round pans and bake for 25 to 30 minutes until a knife comes out smooth when inserted. Cool on a wire rack inside the pans for 5 minutes, and then remove to cool fully. Spread the Coconut Walnut Icing over the top of one of the cakes. Place the second cake on top of it and spread another layer of frosting. Garnish with chopped walnuts if you like.

THE HANGOVER CURE (aka CARROT CAKE)

I call this the hangover cake because after a night of fun and nutrient loss, this dessert will inject a big dose of vitamins back into your system. Plus, you can eat this for breakfast (hey, it's got tons of carrots so it's healthy, silly!), perfect for the morning of recovery. Makes me want to go to the champagne bar with one of my favorite friends, Janet, and put this cake to the test.

Makes 8 slices

DRY

2 ¼ c/371 g Cara's All-Purpose Blend (page 166)

1 ¼ c/275 g packed brown sugar

2 tsp/7.5 g baking powder

2 tsp/5 g cinnamon

1 tsp baking soda

1 tsp ground ginger

½ tsp nutmeg

1 tsp xanthan gum

¾ c/90 g walnuts, chopped

WET

2 ½ c/250 g finely grated carrot

½ c/120 ml vegetable oil

½ c/122 g applesauce

½ c/120 ml orange juice

1 Tbsp/15 ml apple cider vinegar (or lemon juice)

ADD-ONS

1 batch Cream Cheese Frosting (page 155)

1 c/120 g walnuts, chopped

Preheat oven to 350°F/180°C. Lightly grease an 8 x 4-inch/20 x 10-cm loaf pan.

In a large bowl, mix all of the dry ingredients (except walnuts) together. In a medium bowl, thoroughly mix the wet ingredients together. Pour wet ingredients into the dry, and then mix with a wooden spoon until just combined. Fold in the walnuts. Pour batter into the loaf pan.

Bake for 50 to 60 minutes until a toothpick comes out smooth when inserted. Cool on a wire rack inside the pan for 5 minutes, and then remove to cool fully. Once completely cooled, slice the loaf in half horizontally to create 2 layers.

Coat the top of one of the halves with my Cream Cheese Frosting. Place the other half on top and coat the entire loaf with the remainder of the Cream Cheese Frosting. Top with chopped walnuts.

WHITEOUT CAKE

I feel like taking a sled and riding down this cake; it's like a winter wonderland. A white cake filled with coconut, topped with a frosting infused with more coconut, one slice of this white mountain is sure to please the coconut lover in your inner circle.

MAKES 8 SLICES OR 12 CUPCAKES

DRY
2 ½ c/413 g Cara's All-Purpose Blend (page 166)

1 c/200 g granulated sugar

2 tsp/7.5 g baking powder

1 tsp baking soda

½ tsp salt

1 c/60 g shredded coconut

WET
1 ½ c/398 ml full fat coconut milk, canned

¼ c/60 ml hot water

6 Tbsp/90 g applesauce

1 Tbsp/15 ml apple cider vinegar (or lemon juice)

½ tsp vanilla extract

ADD-ON
1 batch Coconut-Dream Frosting (page 156)

Preheat oven to 350°F/180°C and grease two 8-inch/20-cm round cake pans.

In a large bowl, whisk together the dry ingredients. In a medium bowl, combine the wet until well mixed. Pour the wet ingredients into the dry ingredients and stir with a wooden spoon until just combined. Pour evenly into the cake pans.

Bake for 25 to 30 minutes until a toothpick comes out clean when placed in the middle. Cool on a wire rack inside the pans for 5 minutes, and then remove to cool fully. Spread the middle layer and fully frost with Coconut-Dream Frosting.

Chocolate "Soufflés" Individual Cakes

My original intention was to create a beautiful lava cake, but the moment I took these out of the oven, I knew I had embarked on something magical. The rise in these cakes had me in awe, but I then giggled like a schoolgirl when they collapsed in the middle. The real test was the flavor. A crunchy exterior and a soft middle, I feel like I accomplished a complementary vegan soufflé, just for you.

MAKES 2 INDIVIDUAL CAKES

DRY

½ c/83 g Cara's All-Purpose Blend (page 166)

¼ c/37 g lightly packed brown sugar

1 Tbsp/5 g cocoa powder

½ tsp baking powder

WET

¼ c/60 ml hot water

3 Tbsp/33 g melted nondairy chocolate chips plus 1 tsp coconut oil

1 Tbsp/15 g applesauce

½ tsp vanilla extract

2 Tbsp/22 g nondairy chocolate chips

ADD-ONS

Powdered sugar

Fresh berries

Coconut Whipped Cream (page 150)

Preheat oven to 375°F/190°C. Grease two 7-ounce/200-ml ramekins.

Whisk the dry ingredients together in a medium bowl. In a small bowl, combine the wet ingredients. Add into the dry ingredients and mix until just combined.

Place less than half of the batter into the ramekins, and then place 1 tablespoon/11 g of the nondairy chocolate chips in the middle of each cake. Top off with the remainder of the batter. Bake for 15 to 18 minutes or until firm on the top. The middle should have a nice rise to it.

Allow to cool for 5 minutes to allow the middle to collapse. Place on a small plate while still inside the ramekin and garnish with powdered sugar, fresh berries or Coconut Whipped Cream.

The Pink Lady

Perfect for that Grease-themed party (wait, those don't happen anymore?) the Pink Lady is perfect for the girl in your life who loves all things pink! Was that too obvious? Want to make this an even more pinkish delight? Add 3 teaspoons/15 ml of homemade Pink Food Coloring (page 158) to the batter, and then decorate the final product with homemade Pink Sprinkles (page 161). I'm squealing over all the pink-ness already.

Makes 8 slices

DRY
2 ½ c/413 g Cara's All-Purpose Blend (page 166)
1 c/200 g granulated sugar
2 tsp/7.5 g baking powder
1 tsp baking soda
1 tsp xanthan gum
½ tsp salt

WET
1 ½ c/398 ml coconut milk, canned
¼ c/60 ml hot water
6 Tbsp/90 g applesauce
1 Tbsp/15 ml apple cider vinegar (or lemon juice)
½ tsp vanilla extract

ADD-ONS
1 batch Cream Cheese Frosting (page 155)
All-natural food coloring (page 158)

Preheat oven to 350°F/180°C and grease two 8-inch/20-cm round cake pans.

In a large bowl, whisk together the dry ingredients. In a medium bowl, combine the wet until well mixed. Pour the wet ingredients into the dry ingredients and stir with a wooden spoon until just combined. Pour batter evenly into the two pans.

Bake for 25 to 30 minutes or until a toothpick comes out clean when placed in the middle.

Cool on a wire rack inside the pans for 5 minutes and then remove to cool fully. Once cooled, ice with my Cream Cheese Frosting that has been colored with my pink all-natural food coloring.

Blueberry Buttermilk Coffee Cake

I love those mornings when my typical oatmeal doesn't satisfy and I make a beautiful coffee cake. I love how I just lied to you, as if I really like to eat oatmeal. I don't at all. I'd rather eat coffee cake every morning, if I could. There is nothing better than a warm slice, straight out of the oven, with a freshly brewed cup of coffee. The blueberries in this cake burst with juice with each bite—it's addicting.

Makes 8 squares

WET

1 c/240 ml nondairy milk

1 Tbsp/15 ml apple cider vinegar (or lemon juice)

¼ c/60 ml vegetable oil

FOR THE SUGAR TOPPING

3 Tbsp/10 g Cara's All-Purpose Blend (page 166)

⅓ c/48 g lightly packed brown sugar

1 Tbsp/13 g granulated sugar

2 tsp/5 g cinnamon

Pinch of salt

2 Tbsp/28 g vegan butter, melted

DRY

2 c/330 g Cara's All-Purpose Blend (page 166)

¾ c/125 g granulated sugar

3 tsp/11 g baking powder

1 tsp xanthan gum

½ tsp salt

ADD-IN

1 c/140 g fresh blueberries

Preheat oven to 350°F/180°C. Grease an 8 x 8-inch/20 x 20-cm square pan.

Mix nondairy milk and vinegar together and let sit for 5 to 7 minutes to sour.

For the sugar topping, combine the flour, sugars, cinnamon and salt in a small bowl. Cut in the cold vegan butter and blend into the mix until small crumbles form. You might have to use your fingers to blend. Set aside.

Combine all of the dry ingredients. Whisk well. Pour oil into soured nondairy milk and pour into dry ingredients, stirring with a wooden spoon until just combined. Fold in the blueberries. Pour into the greased pan and coat with the sugar topping.

Bake for 25 to 30 minutes. Allow the pan to cool on a wire rack and serve warm.

Cinnamon Streusel Coffee Cake

This is a recipe of my childhood. Of course the only baking from scratch that I ever did as a teenager was from a mix, but nevertheless, coffee cake was my specialty. I was darn good at opening that box and mixing in oil. It must be the cinnamon and sugar that hooks me every time, but in my opinion the higher the streusel is stacked, the better!

Makes 8 squares

FOR THE CINNAMON STREUSEL FILLING

1 ¾ c/289 g Cara's All-Purpose Blend (page 166)

1 c/220 g brown sugar, packed

1 ¼ tsp/3 g cinnamon

¼ tsp salt

¾ c/168 g vegan butter, cold and cut into small pieces

1 ½ c/180 g chopped toasted pecans

DRY

2 c/330 g Cara's All-Purpose Blend (page 166)

½ c/73 g lightly packed brown sugar

3 tsp/11 g baking powder

1 tsp xanthan gum

½ tsp salt

WET

1 c/240 ml nondairy milk

¼ c/60 ml vegetable oil

1 Tbsp/15 ml apple cider vinegar (or lemon juice)

FOR THE GLAZE

1 c/120 g powdered sugar

2 Tbsp/30 ml nondairy milk

ADD-ON

½ batch Royal Icing (page 158)

Preheat oven to 350°F/180°C. Grease an 8 x 8-inch/20 x 20-cm square pan.

For the cinnamon streusel filling, combine the flour, brown sugar, cinnamon and salt in a small bowl. Cut in the cold vegan butter and pecans and blend into the mix until small crumbles form. You might have to use your fingers to blend. Set aside.

In a large bowl whisk together all of the dry ingredients for the cake. Make a well in the center and pour in all of the wet ingredients. With a wooden spoon stir until just combined. Spoon half the batter into a greased pan. Sprinkle half the streusel filling mixture evenly over the batter. Top with remaining batter and spread evenly. Sprinkle remaining streusel topping mixture evenly over batter.

Bake 25 to 30 minutes or until knife comes out clean when inserted in the middle. Cool the pan on a wire rack and let it sit for a few minutes. Drizzle the top of the cake with half a batch of the Royal Icing and serve.

Chocolate Icebox Cake

Not only are you going to love how easy this cake is to make, you are going to slap yourself when you realize how silky and chocolaty it is. The best part is when you find a chocolate chip to chomp down on, giving this cake a fun texture.

Makes 8 slices

2 (14-oz [414-ml]) cans of coconut cream, refrigerated overnight

½ c/60 g powdered sugar

½ c/44 g cocoa powder

1 tsp vanilla extract

36 Grandma's Chocolate Chip Cookies (page 37) or use a crunchy cookie of choice

Chocolate shavings (for garnish)

With an electric mixer, mix the coconut cream, sugar and cocoa powder together until soft peaks form (this will take 3-5 minutes). Add vanilla extract and mix briefly. If you are having troubles with it stiffening, simply place it into the freezer for 5 to 10 minutes to chill after you have combined everything together.

Line a 9-inch/22.5-cm springform pan with the first layer of cookies. Break the cookies into pieces to fit open spaces (no need to worry about it covering perfectly, though).

For the second layer, scoop the chocolate cream on top of the cookies (enough to just coat).

Layer the cake with more cookies. Repeat until you are out of cookies, cream or you have reached the top of the pan (whichever comes first).

Place into the fridge for 2 to 3 hours or until set. Remove from the pan and garnish with shaved chocolate. Slice, serve and enjoy.

Lazy Man's Tiramisu

The only difficult thing about this recipe is waiting for the cans of coconut cream to chill completely. I was never one for patience. The amazing thing about this recipe is how the cream absorbs moisture into the crunchy cookies and makes them soft, reminiscent of ladyfingers, without the hassle of baking them from scratch.

Makes 8 slices

3 dozen Chocolate Cloud cookies (page 41) or chocolate cookie of choice

1 recipe for Rum Whipped Cream (see below)

1 recipe for Espresso Whipped Cream (see below)

FOR THE RUM WHIPPED CREAM

1 (14-oz [414-ml]) can coconut cream, refrigerated overnight

½ c/60 g powdered sugar

1 Tbsp/15 ml dark rum

FOR THE ESPRESSO WHIPPED CREAM

1 (14-oz [414-ml]) can coconut cream, refrigerated overnight

½ c/60 g powdered sugar

1 Tbsp/6 g cocoa powder

1 Tbsp/8 g instant espresso powder

1 Tbsp/15 ml strongly brewed coffee

For the rum whipped cream

Open the can of coconut cream (do your best not to shake or vigorously move it). Scoop the top thick layer into a medium-sized deep bowl. If the cream has been chilled long enough, you can use the majority of the can's contents.

Combine the powdered sugar with an electric mixer on medium speed until fluffy, 3 to 5 minutes. Add rum and beat another 30 seconds. (You can always place in the freezer if it is not stiffening up.)

For the espresso whipped cream

Open the can of coconut cream (do your best not to shake or vigorously move it). Scoop the top thick layer into a medium-sized deep bowl. If the cream has been chilled long enough, you can use the majority of the can's contents.

Combine the powdered sugar, cocoa powder and instant espresso with an electric mixer on medium speed until fluffy, 3 to 5 minutes. Add the coffee and beat another 30 seconds. (You can always place in the freezer if it is not stiffening up.)

To assemble

Line a 9-inch/22.5-cm springform pan with the first layer of cookies. Break the cookies into pieces to fit open spaces (no need to worry about it covering perfectly, though). For the second layer, scoop the rum cream on top of the cookies, just enough to coat.

Layer the cake with more cookies and then layer with the espresso cream. Repeat until you are out of cookies, cream or you have reached the top of the pan (whichever comes first). Place into the fridge for 2 to 3 hours or until set. Remove from the pan and dust with cocoa powder. Slice, serve and enjoy.

Strawberry Swirl Cheesecake with Chocolate Graham Cracker Crust

I was never one for cheesecake. It just never held my attention like, say, brownies did. That is until I started to experiment with the incredible cashew—a food that could be made into almost anything. I became a cheesecake believer. The creamy flavor that cashews give this recipe is mind-blowing—you would never guess that the filling is made from nuts.

Makes 8 slices

FOR THE CRUST
1 ½ c/390 g Gluten-Free Graham Crackers, crushed (page 49)

⅓ c/75 g vegan butter, melted

¼ c/50 g granulated sugar

2 Tbsp/28 g brown sugar, packed

1 Tbsp/6 g cocoa powder

FOR THE CHEESECAKE FILLING
3 ½ c/896 g cashews, soaked for 2 to 3 hours

¼ c/60 ml lemon juice

½ c/120 ml agave nectar

2 tsp/10 ml vanilla extract

1 tsp lemon zest

½ c/120 ml unrefined coconut oil, melted

FOR THE STRAWBERRY SWIRL
2 ½ c/570 g frozen strawberries, thawed and puréed (two 10-oz/570-g bags)

¼ c/50 g granulated sugar

ADD-ONS
Fresh strawberries

1 batch Coconut Whipped Cream (page 150)

Preheat oven to 350°F/180°C. Grease a 9-inch/22.5-cm round springform pan.

Combine all of the crust ingredients until well combined. Press into pan and bake for 10 to 12 minutes. Allow to cool fully before pouring in the filling. In a blender, combine all the filling ingredients except for the coconut oil until completely smooth. If it is difficult to blend, add 1 tablespoon/15 ml of water at a time until the mix is able to blend properly. Try not to add too much, though—you want a thick filling. Add the oil and blend until combined.

Pour over the crust. Combine the sugar and strawberry purée to make the swirl. Then, pour the strawberry swirl over the cheesecake and use a spoon to gently swirl it into the filling. Place in the fridge for several hours until firm. (You might need to freeze the pie for a few minutes before you take it out of the pan.)

Serve with fresh strawberries and homemade Coconut Whipped Cream.

chapter 5

Breads & Pastries

The most difficult food group to recreate in the allergen-friendly world is bread. It can be a bit intimidating because there are new rules when it comes to baking gluten-, egg- and dairy-free. But patience and perseverance in the kitchen is greatly rewarded in this chapter. Stick with it and keep trying if at first you don't get it. There is nothing more rewarding than watching the dough rise the way it does in my Cinnamon Raisin Loaf. Before you know it you will be a pro, creating tasty breads like the Yeasted Banana Cardamom Bread in this chapter. Who knows, maybe you will be teaching me a thing or two in no time . . .

Pocket Pastry Dough

This is a simpler version of the typical melt-in-your-mouth pastry dough. Whereas most pastry requires you to refrigerate the dough for hours on end, the Pocket Pastry Dough doesn't require a lot of time for chilling. Though it doesn't quite yield the same end product as a croissant, this dough still packs a buttery, flakey bite.

Makes 8 pocket pastries

2 ¼ tsp/7 g dry active yeast

½ c/120 ml warm water

2 Tbsp/26 g granulated sugar

¼ c/60 ml coconut milk, canned

½ c/120 ml nondairy milk, warmed

¼ c/48 g ground white chia seeds

¼ c/48 g ground psyllium husk

2 ¼ c/371 g Cara's Special Blend (page 166)

¼ tsp salt

¾ c/168 g vegan butter

¾ c/168 g non-hydrogenated shortening

Pour the yeast into the warm water with 1 teaspoon of the sugar and let sit for 10 minutes until frothy. Pour the coconut milk, nondairy milk, chia seeds and ground psyllium husk into the yeast mix. It will thicken up within 2 minutes.

Whisk together the flour blend, remainder of the sugar and salt together in a large bowl. Cut in the butter and shortening until small lumps form and is evenly distributed. Mix the yeast mixture into the flour mix with a wooden spoon until a dough forms. It should not be too sticky. If it is, add 1 teaspoon of flour blend at a time until you can handle the dough.

Cover the top of the bowl with the dough inside with plastic wrap and set in a warm, dry place in your kitchen for 60 minutes or until doubled in size.

Sweet Dough

A great base to use in pastry making, this Sweet Dough makes a soft yet chewy bite. Try interchanging the dough for the Pocket Pastries (page 122) and Sweet Almond Braided Bread (page 129). You might find a new texture you like better. It's all about experimentation, right?

2 CUPS/460 G

2 ¼ tsp/7 g dry active yeast
¼ c/60 ml warm nondairy milk
¼ c/50 g granulated sugar
2 Tbsp/24 g ground white chia seeds plus ½ c/120 ml warm water
¾ tsp salt
1 tsp xanthan gum
4 Tbsp/48 g vegan butter, melted
2 ½ c/248 g Cara's All-Purpose Blend (page 166)

Proof the yeast by placing the entire contents of the packet into a bowl with the nondairy milk and a pinch of sugar. Allow to set for 5 to 10 minutes until it becomes frothy.

Pour the yeast mix and chia seeds soaked in water into a large bowl. Using an electric mixer beat for 30 seconds. Add sugar, salt, xanthan gum and butter. With a wooden spoon, add the flour blend until just combined.

Cover to rise in a warm place for 30 to 45 minutes.

ALMOND POCKET PASTRIES

Buttery, flakey, with a soft bite, these treats were difficult to name initially. Not quite
as fluffy as a croissant, so I couldn't call it that, yet not as delicate as a hand pie. So I went
onto Facebook (where all decisions are made) and asked my readers to come up with a good name.
Thankfully Salina Anderson came up with the great name Pocket Pastries. A winner was found!
(I must add that Cadry of Cadry's Kitchen does deserve honorable mention for her idea of
Pastry Pouches. It was a tough call but the people have spoken.)

MAKES 8 POCKET PASTRIES

1 batch Pocket Pastry Dough (page 122)

FOR THE ALMOND FILLING
⅔ c/80 g almonds
2 Tbsp/25 g brown sugar
1 Tbsp/15 ml water
½ tsp almond extract

FOR THE "EGG" WASH, FULLY MIX
TOGETHER
1 Tbsp/15 ml water
1 tsp cornstarch

FOR THE TOPPING
Sliced almonds
Powdered sugar

In a high-speed blender combine all of the filling ingredients until a thick paste is
created. You will need to scrape the sides often. If you are still having difficulties
with blending, add 1 tablespoon/15 ml of water at a time until desired consistency
is reached.

Once you have let your Pocket Pastry Dough double in size, divide into 2 even
balls. Between 2 pieces of parchment paper, roll the dough out into a trimmed
12 x 6-inch/30 x 15-cm rectangle. Cut the dough horizontally in half to separate
the rectangle into 2, and then cut out 3 x 3-inch/7.5 x 7.5-cm squares. You should
have eight 3 x 3-inch/7.5 x 7.5-cm squares at this point.

Place approximately 1 tablespoon/15 ml of almond filling in the middle of 4
dough squares. With a metal spatula, gently place the other 4 squares on top
and seal the edges with your fingers. Trim with a knife if needed. Repeat with
the other ball of dough until you have 8 total pockets. Place on a parchment
paper–lined baking sheet and set for another 20 minutes.

Preheat oven to 375°F/190°C.

Brush the tops of the dough with the "egg" wash and immediately cover with
sliced almonds. Bake for 18 to 20 minutes until tops are lightly browned. Garnish
with powdered sugar. Best if served warm.

CARA'S TIP: For chocolate-filled pockets, replace the almond
filling with 1 tablespoon/15 g of nondairy chocolate chips
per pocket. Coat with the "egg" wash before placing into the
oven and bake for 18 to 20 minutes. Once they have slightly
cooled out of the oven, drizzle the tops with melted chocolate.
Serve warm.

Creamy "Cheese" Pastry Squares

These almost bite-sized pastries fit perfectly between two fingers as you nibble on just the right amount of sweetness. Make sure you keep your pinky finger out while eating each dainty bite—your friends will surely be impressed by your sophistication. Serve with a drizzle of icing and a nice cup of tea.

Makes 12 pastry squares

Sweet Dough recipe (page 123)

FOR THE CREAM FILLING
6 Tbsp/88 g vegan cream cheese
1 Tbsp/14 g powdered sugar
2 tsp/6.5 g cornstarch
1 tsp lemon juice
¼ tsp vanilla extract
¼ tsp almond extract

FOR THE "EGG" WASH, FULLY MIX TOGETHER
1 Tbsp/15 ml water
1 tsp cornstarch

1 batch Royal Icing (page 158)

Once you have let your dough double in size, divide into 3 balls. Between 2 pieces of parchment paper, roll the dough out into a trimmed 12 x 6-inch/30 x 15-cm rectangle that is ¼ inch/6 mm thick. Cut the dough horizontally in half to separate the rectangle into 2, and then create 3 x 3-inch/7.5 x 7.5-cm squares. You should have eight 3 x 3-inch/7.5 x 7.5-cm squares at this point. With a circle cutter, make holes in the middle of 4 of the squares and place each one on top of each of the remaining squares. Press down with your fingers to seal the edges. Trim if needed. By now you should have a thicker 3 x 3-inch/7.5 x 7.5-cm square with an opening to insert the filling.

In a small bowl, add all the ingredients together for the cream filling until fully combined. With a spoon, place 1 or 2 teaspoons/5-10 g of the filling into the opening of the square, or just enough to fill it. Allow to set for 20 minutes on a parchment paper–lined baking sheet.

Preheat oven to 400°F/200°C.

Lightly brush the "egg" wash onto the pastry, and then bake for 15 to 17 minutes or just until lightly browned. Remove from oven and allow to cool down for 5 minutes, and then drizzle with Royal Icing.

CARA'S TIP: For jam-filled pastry squares, combine ½ cup/145 g jam of choice with 1 teaspoon cornstarch. Place into the square openings, instead of filling with the creamy "cheesy" mix, and bake as instructed.

Sweet Almond Braided Bread

The braided bread of the gods, this soft, chewy, creamy almond-flavored bread will look beautiful on your table for the next ladies brunch. Be sure to gobble it up immediately, though—it tastes best when eaten right out of the oven.

Makes 1 loaf

Sweet Dough Recipe (page 123)

FOR ALMOND CREAM CHEESE FILLING
5 Tbsp/73 g vegan cream cheese
2 Tbsp/8 g powdered sugar
1 Tbsp/10 g Cara's All-Purpose Blend
(page 166)
½ tsp vanilla extract
¼ tsp almond extract

FOR THE ICING
1 c/120 g powdered sugar
2 tsp/10 ml milk
½ tsp almond extract

FOR THE "EGG" WASH, FULLY MIX
TOGETHER
1 Tbsp/15 ml water
1 tsp cornstarch

FOR GARNISHING
¼ c/23 g sliced almonds
Powdered sugar

Preheat oven to 375°F/190°C.

Mix all the filling ingredients together until well combined. Next, roll out dough between 2 pieces of parchment paper into a trimmed 13 x 8-inch/32.5 x 20-cm rectangle. Place cream cheese filling in the center (approximately 2 inches to 3 inches/5 cm to 7.5 cm wide). Make cuts on the long side at 2-inch/5-cm intervals from the edges toward the filling in center.

Alternately fold opposite strips at an angle across the filling until all pieces are done and you have created the look of a braid. Brush with "egg" wash and place on a baking sheet lined with parchment paper. Bake for 20 to 23 minutes until the loaf is lightly browned along the edges. In a small bowl, combine all ingredients for the icing until smooth. Drizzle with icing and sprinkle with almond slices. If desired, dust with powdered sugar. Best if served warm.

Tomato Herb Focaccia Bread

The potato in the recipe gives this bread that secret oomph and moisture it needs to be a fabulous-tasting focaccia. Don't omit it, because it is the star of the ingredients. Feel free to add to the toppings: olives, garlic or even sub the Roma tomatoes for sundried tomatoes. Use this bread as the base for a pizza crust too!

Makes one (8"/20-cm) round

WET
1 tsp instant yeast
¼ c/60 ml warm water
¼ tsp sugar
1 small russet potato, cubed
1 Tbsp/15 ml olive oil

DRY
1 ¾ c/225 g Cara's Special Blend (page 166), plus ¼ c/32 g to reserve
1 tsp xantham gum
1 tsp salt

FOR THE TOPPING
1 Tbsp/15 ml extra virgin olive oil
2 Roma tomatoes, thinly sliced
1 Tbsp/1.7 g fresh rosemary
Coarse sea salt

Place the potato cubes in a small saucepan filled with just enough water to cover them and bring to a boil. Simmer until tender, about 10 minutes. Drain the water and allow to fully cool. Using a cheese grater, collect ¼ cup/42 g lightly packed grated potato.

In a medium bowl, combine the water and yeast with granulated sugar. Allow to froth for 10 minutes.

In a large bowl combine the dry ingredients. Add yeast mix and remainder of the wet ingredients into the dry mix. Stir with a wooden spoon until well-combined. Cover with plastic wrap and let rise in a warm place for one hour, or until doubled in volume.

Preheat the oven to 425°F/220°C.

Line the counter with 2 separate pieces of parchment paper and cover each piece with ¼ cup/32 g reserved flour mix. Yes, you will need that much flour. Divide the dough in half and place each piece on top of the parchment paper. Cover the dough with the flour and begin to gently knead until the flour is absorbed and the dough is not sticky. With your hands, mold each dough piece into an 8-inch/20-cm round.

Place the parchment paper on its own baking sheet. Coat the top of the dough with olive oil, then the sliced tomatoes, fresh rosemary, and coarse salt. Place in the oven for 25 to 30 minutes or until brown.

Cinnamon Raisin Loaf

This beautiful bread is simply magical, just like the slices I used to enjoy as a kid! This bread is soft and pillowy—it's insane that it's gluten-free and vegan. Slice and toast it with a small knob of vegan butter and enjoy it with your coffee.

Makes 1 loaf

WET
1 c/240 ml warm nondairy milk

2 ¼ tsp/7 g active dry yeast

2 tsp/8 g granulated sugar

1 c/240 ml warm water

3 Tbsp/45 ml oil

1 tsp apple cider vinegar (or lemon juice)

3 Tbsp/45 ml maple syrup

5 Tbsp/35 g ground white chia seeds

DRY
3 c/495 g Cara's Special Blend (page 166)

¼ c/30 g buckwheat flour

1 tsp baking powder

½ tsp baking soda

2 tsp/5 g cinnamon

½ tsp salt

½ c/73 g raisins

FOR THE CINNAMON SUGAR FILLING
½ c/73 g lightly packed brown sugar

¼ c/50 g sugar

3 tsp/7.5 g cinnamon

In a medium bowl combine the warmed nondairy milk with the yeast and sugar—allow to proof until frothy, approximately 10 minutes. Add the water, oil, vinegar, syrup and chia seeds into the yeast mix and whisk until well combined. Allow to sit another 2 minutes for the chia to expand.

In a large bowl, whisk together the dry ingredients. Pour the wet ingredients into the dry and stir with a wooden spoon for 1 minute.

In a small bowl, whisk together the ingredients for the cinnamon sugar filling and set aside.

Pour ⅓ of the batter into a greased 8 x 4-inch/20 x 10-cm loaf pan. Sprinkle ½ of the cinnamon sugar mixture over it. Pour another ⅓ of the batter in another layer. Sprinkle the remainder of the cinnamon sugar mix. Pour the remainder of the batter over that last layer. Using the back of a spoon, smooth out the top and gently press down to ensure there are no gaps in the batter. Allow to rise until the loaf rises past the top of the pan (approximately 30 to 45 minutes) in a warm, non-drafty area of your kitchen.

Preheat oven to 350°F/180°C.

Place the loaf in the oven on the middle rack and bake for 60 minutes until the top springs back when you touch it. Allow to cool in the pan briefly until you can remove it from the pan and transfer it to cool completely on a wire rack.

CARA'S TIP: Make sure that you don't cut into the loaf for at least 2 to 3 hours after taking it out of the oven. It will be tempting to do so sooner, but the longer you allow for cooling, the more the inside will be completely baked.

Yeasted Banana Cardamom Bread

Banana bread but hopped up on yeast. It's the kind of bread that if my mom were here with me, I'd bake a loaf for us to eat over a big cup of coffee (though she likes hers a bit stronger than I do) while we giggled over movie quotes. Well, really, it would be me making fun of her trying to quote movies but just scrambling up the words instead. I love her regardless.

Makes 1 loaf

WET

¾ c/180 ml warm water

2 ¼ tsp/7 g active dry yeast

½ c/100 ml sugar

¾ c/170 g mashed banana (approximately 3 small ripe bananas)

¾ c/180 ml warm nondairy milk

3 Tbsp/45 ml oil

1 tsp vanilla extract

½ c/60 g walnuts, chopped

DRY

2 c/330 g Cara's Special Blend (page 166)

¼ c/30 g buckwheat flour

½ c/73 g lightly packed brown sugar

5 Tbsp/30 g ground psyllium husk

4 Tbsp/28 g ground white chia seed

1 tsp cinnamon

½ tsp nutmeg

½ tsp ground cardamom

½ tsp salt

In a medium bowl combine ½ cup/120 ml water with the yeast and sugar—allow to proof until frothy. Add the remainder of the wet ingredients into the yeast mix and stir until well combined.

In a large bowl, whisk together the dry ingredients. Pour the wet ingredients into the dry and stir with a wooden spoon until just combined. Cover with a towel and allow it to double in size, about 1 hour.

Lightly grease an 8 x 4-inch/20 x 10-cm loaf pan.

Pour the batter into the loaf pan and allow to rise again until the loaf rises past the top of the pan, approximately 30 minutes.

Preheat oven to 350°F/180°C.

Place the loaf in the oven on the middle rack and bake for 60 minutes. Place a piece of tinfoil over the top and continue to bake for another 25 minutes until a knife comes out clean when inserted. Allow to cool in the pan until easy to touch, and then transfer to a wire rack until it has completely cooled.

Rosemary Beer Bread "Cupcakes"

So is this where I admit that I am deeply in love with beer and I will go to any length just to infuse it into my baked goods? I think I've said too much already.

Makes 12 muffins

DRY

2 ¼ c/371 g Cara's All-Purpose Blend
(page 166)
2 Tbsp/28 g granulated sugar
1 Tbsp/1.7 g dried rosemary
2 tsp/7.5 g baking powder
½ tsp baking soda
¼ tsp salt

WET

1 (12-oz [356-g]) gluten-free beer of choice
2 Tbsp/28 g vegan butter, melted

Preheat oven to 375°F/190°C. Grease or line a muffin pan.

In a large bowl, whisk together the dry ingredients. Making a well in the center of the mix, pour the beer and melted vegan butter in and stir gently with a wooden spoon. Pour batter into the muffin pan.

Bake 23 to 25 minutes until a toothpick comes out dry when inserted. Allow to cool slightly in the pan, then transfer to a wire rack.

Stone-Ground Cornbread

Doesn't the image of cornbread make you want to whip up a big batch of veggie chili and eat it snuggled up under a blanket? (Maybe I'm just hungry.) There are so many things you can do to this recipe to spice it up too. Add chopped jalapeños, some vegan shredded cheddar cheese or even drained green chilies to make this hearty cornbread even better.

Makes 8 slices

DRY

1 c/165 g Cara's All-Purpose Blend (page 166)

1 ¼ c/153 g stone-ground yellow cornmeal

½ c/100 g granulated sugar

3 tsp/11 g baking powder

½ tsp salt

WET

3 tsp/9.5 g Ener-G Egg Replacer plus 6 Tbsp/90 ml water, whisk until frothy

1 c/120 ml nondairy milk

4 Tbsp/56 g vegan butter

Preheat oven to 400°F/ 200°C and grease an 8-inch/20-cm round pan.

Combine the dry ingredients in a medium bowl. Make a well in the center and pour the wet ingredients into the well. Mix until just combined. Pour batter into the greased pan and bake for 20 to 25 minutes until the top is lightly browned.

Drown in nondairy butter.

Pumpkin Streusel Bread

This is by far one of the tastiest quick breads I've ever made. If I could, I would make this every day. Not only is the flavor spot-on, but it is so super-moist it will melt in your mouth with each bite. Don't believe me? Try it out for yourself.

Makes 1 loaf or 8 slices

DRY

2 c/330 g Cara's All-Purpose Blend (page 166)

½ c/110 g brown sugar, packed

½ c/100 g granulated sugar

2 tsp/7.5 g baking powder

1 tsp baking soda

1 ½ tsp/5 g xanthan gum

1 ½ tsp/2.5 g cinnamon

¼ tsp nutmeg

¼ tsp ground cloves (optional)

½ tsp salt

WET

1 c/245 g canned pumpkin purée (not the pie mix)

½ c/120 ml oil

½ c/120 ml hot water

ADD-INS

½ c/60 g walnuts, chopped (optional)

Raw pepitas for garnishing the top (optional)

Preheat oven to 350°F/180°C. Lightly grease an 8 x 4-inch/20 x 10-cm loaf pan.

In a large bowl, mix all of the dry ingredients together. In a medium bowl, thoroughly mix the wet ingredients together. Pour wet ingredients into the dry and mix with a wooden spoon until just combined. Fold in the walnuts. Pour batter into the loaf pan (if garnishing, place pepitas on top of batter).

Bake for 50 to 60 minutes until knife comes out smooth when inserted. Allow to cool for 10 minutes and transfer to a cooling rack.

Dark Chocolate Quick Bread

I created the perfect combo of food groups in this loaf: chocolate and bread. The only thing that would make it even more perfect is if I figured out a way to incorporate coffee into it. Instead, I just offer up the simple solution to eat a slice with a cup of freshly brewed coffee. There. Perfection.

Makes 1 loaf or 8 slices

DRY

2 c/330 g Cara's Special Blend (page 166)

1 c/220 g brown sugar, packed

¼ c/22 g dark cocoa powder

2 tsp/7.5 g baking powder

1 tsp baking soda

1 ½ tsp/5 g xanthan gum

½ tsp salt

WET

1 c/245 g canned pumpkin purée
(not the pie mix)

½ c/120 ml oil

½ c/120 ml warm nondairy milk

ADD-IN

¾ c/132 g nondairy dark chocolate chips

Preheat oven to 350°F/180°C. Lightly grease an 8 x 4-inch/20 x 10-cm loaf pan.

In a large bowl, mix all of the dry ingredients together. In a medium bowl, thoroughly mix the wet ingredients together. Pour wet ingredients into the dry and mix with a wooden spoon until just combined. Fold in the chocolate chips and pour batter into the loaf pan.

Bake for 50 to 60 minutes until knife comes out smooth when inserted. Allow to cool for 10 minutes and transfer to a cooling rack.

Spiced Zucchini Loaf

Full of spices and rich in zucchini, this melt-in-your-mouth quick bread makes a perfect breakfast or midday treat.

Makes 1 loaf or 8 slices

DRY

2 ¼ c/371 g Cara's All-Purpose Blend (page 166)

½ c/110 g brown sugar, packed

½ c/100 g granulated sugar

2 tsp/7.5 g baking powder

1 tsp baking soda

1 ½ tsp/5 g xanthan gum

2 tsp/5 g cinnamon

½ tsp ground ginger

½ tsp cardamom

¼ tsp nutmeg

½ tsp salt

WET

1 c/124 g finely shredded zucchini (approximately 1 ½ medium zucchinis)

½ c/120 ml vegetable oil

½ c/120 ml hot water

ADD-IN

½ c/60 g walnuts, chopped

Preheat oven to 350°F/180°C. Lightly grease an 8 x 4-inch/20-cm loaf pan.

In a large bowl, mix all of the dry ingredients together. In a medium bowl, thoroughly mix the wet ingredients together. Pour wet ingredients into the dry and mix with a wooden spoon until just combined. Fold in the walnuts. Pour the batter into the loaf pan.

Bake for 50 to 60 minutes until knife comes out smooth when inserted. Allow to cool for 10 minutes and transfer to a cooling rack.

Frosted Gingerbread Loaf

Oh the crystallized ginger! Reminds me of my dear friend Lina (whom I prefer to call Blondie). Thanks to her exposing me to this delectable treat, I could eat this type of ginger straight from the package. (In fact, I think I even learned that behavior from Blondie, herself.) This cake is just for her.

Makes 1 loaf or 8 slices

DRY
2 ¼ c/371 g Cara's All-Purpose Blend (page 166)

½ c/73 g lightly packed brown sugar

2 tsp/7.5 g baking powder

1 tsp baking soda

1 ½ tsp/4 g ground ginger

1 tsp cinnamon

¼ tsp nutmeg

½ tsp salt

WET
¾ c/184 g pumpkin purée, canned (not the pumpkin pie mix)

½ c/120 ml vegetable oil

½ c/120 ml nondairy milk

½ c/120 ml molasses

FOR THE TOPPING
1 batch Cream Cheese Frosting (page 155)

¼ c/40 g chopped crystallized ginger

Preheat oven to 350°F/180°C. Grease an 8 x 4-inch/20 x 10-cm loaf pan.

Whisk together the dry ingredients in a large bowl. In a medium bowl, combine the wet ingredients and pour into the dry. Stir with a wooden spoon until just combined. Spoon the batter into the greased pan.

Bake for 45 to 50 minutes until a knife comes out smooth when inserted. Allow to cool for 10 minutes in the pan before transferring to a wire rack to cool completely.

Frost with the Cream Cheese Frosting and chopped crystallized ginger.

chapter 6

SAUCES, TOPPINGS & FROSTINGS

~~~~~~

No dessert tastes good unless it is accompanied by a homemade caramel sauce or topping of whipped cream made from coconut milk. Anyone else having flashbacks to the days of spraying the aerosol can of whipped cream directly into your mouth? Here is a treasure trove of how to make delicious drizzles like the Sweet Sauce to accompany a fresh batch of warm brownies or a variety of frostings to coat your cupcakes. And don't forget the homemade food colorings and sprinkles! This chapter is sure to delight the kid within.

WARMED-UP CARAMEL SAUCE

One of the things that I do not like about most vegan caramel is the flavor most vegan butters impart. However, there is something beautiful that happens when you add nut butter; it adds a certain creamy smoothness that really makes this sauce shine. This caramel sauce is so simple to make—it's one of my readers' favorites, as well as my own.

MAKES ½ CUP/200 G SAUCE

⅓ c/75 g vegan butter
⅓ c/82 ml light corn syrup
⅔ c/133 g vegan sugar
3 Tbsp/45 ml water
⅓ c/86 g creamy peanut butter (almond or sunflower butter works fine)

Combine all of the ingredients in a small saucepan and bring to a boil. Turn heat down to medium-low and stir constantly.

Allow to boil for 5 minutes or until the sauce turns a beautiful golden color. Be sure not to burn it (you will know by the smell). If you are using a candy thermometer, cook just until a little after the soft ball phase, 250°F/120°C.

Pour into an airtight glass jar with the lid off to cool down completely. You can store in the refrigerator for up to 1 week.

Date Caramel Sauce

If you have not entered into the world of raw foods, this recipe is a great place to start! It shows you just how easy and tasty working with natural foods can be. If you have ever had a date (not the kind involving dinner and a movie, silly—I mean the fruit) you know that it already has a creamy, caramel-like flavor to it. This is why it makes the best base for this raw caramel sauce. Blend up a batch of this raw sauce and see if you can taste the difference.

Makes ¼ cup/80 g sauce

8 large Medjool dates, pits removed (soaked in water for 1 hour or more)

2 Tbsp/30 ml water

2 Tbsp/30 ml agave nectar or maple syrup (add more if you have a sweet tooth)

2 Tbsp/30 ml unrefined coconut oil, melted

½ tsp vanilla extract

Drain the water from the dates.

Mix all ingredients in a high-speed blender for 3 to 5 minutes or until smooth. If it's too thick, add 1 teaspoon water at a time. You want it thick enough to blend but not runny.

Place in the fridge to cool and thicken.

CARA'S TIP: You don't need to break your wallet by buying a Vitamix to make a smooth caramel sauce from dates, but you will need a high-speed blender. I have the Cuisinart version of the Magic Bullet and it's not only affordable but works wonders for blending!

Homemade Chocolate Sauce

If you are anything like me, the thought of getting in your car to buy a bottle of chocolate syrup at 8 p.m. to accompany that big bowl of nondairy ice cream sounds exhausting. Too many things to do—put on shoes, find keys, walk to the car, etc. In fact, laziness was the exact motivation and inspiration behind this very recipe. This is the perfect homemade chocolate sauce that gives you the perfect excuse not to get off your couch at night.

Makes approximately ¼ cup/150 g sauce

¼ c/22 g dark cocoa powder

2 Tbsp/16 g powdered sugar

4 Tbsp/56 g coconut oil or vegan shortening, melted

1 tsp vanilla

Combine all ingredients in a small bowl. Place into a pouring bottle and chill in the refrigerator to thicken up a little bit.

The more coconut oil you add, the thicker the syrup will be. If the syrup is too cold and thickens up too much, simply place the closed pouring bottle into a bowl of hot water until it melts.

The Sweet Sauce

This sauce is a purée of your favorite berries with a dash of lemon juice to give it a little zing. It goes perfectly with any chocolate dish. Brownies, soufflés, cake—drizzle it over anything, really, to balance out the sweetness.

Makes ½ cup/70 g sauce

1 c/140 g frozen berries of choice

1 Tbsp/15 ml water

2 Tbsp/12.5 g sugar

Juice of 1 lemon wedge

Bring everything but the lemon juice to a boil in a small saucepan, stirring occasionally and allowing the sugar to dissolve.

Remove from heat and place in a blender. Mix until smooth. If you do not like the seeds, strain through a fine-mesh strainer. Squeeze the lemon juice in and stir.

Serve warm or refrigerate until chilled.

Coconut Whipped Cream

The concept of whipped cream from the cream of the coconut is not my original idea. Whoever came up with this genius idea is, well, a genius! If you do not have store-bought available, here is my take on this easy-to-make and oh-so delicious coconut whipped cream.

Makes approximately 2 cups/120 g

1 (14-oz [414-ml]) can coconut cream, refrigerated overnight or longer

5 Tbsp/50 g powdered sugar

1 tsp vanilla extract

Open the can (do your best not to shake or vigorously move it). Scoop the top thick layer into a medium-sized deep bowl. If the cream has been chilled long enough, you can use the majority of the can's content—the beauty of using coconut cream.

Combine the powdered sugar with an electric mixer on medium speed until fluffy, 3 to 5 minutes. Add vanilla extract and beat another 30 seconds. (You can always place in the freezer if it is not stiffening up.)

Stores beautifully in an airtight container for 2 to 3 weeks.

CARA'S TIP: I keep several cans of coconut cream in my fridge for that special day when I do decide to make whipped cream. This way I don't have to chill it overnight and wait (I hate waiting). It's especially convenient because each can varies in the amount of chilled cream it disperses. If you don't get a lot from one can (or if it didn't set properly for God knows what reason) you will always have another one handy and ready to go.

Chocolate Dream Whipped Cream

1 (14-oz [414-ml]) can coconut cream, refrigerated overnight or longer

4 Tbsp/24 g powdered sugar

3 Tbsp/17 g cocoa powder

1 tsp coffee liqueur (or vanilla extract)

Open the can (do your best not to shake or vigorously move it). Scoop the top thick layer into a medium-sized deep bowl. If the cream has been chilled long enough, you can use the majority of the can's content—the beauty of using coconut cream.

Combine the powdered sugar and cocoa powder with an electric mixer on medium speed until fluffy, 3 to 5 minutes. Add coffee liqueur and beat for another 30 seconds. (You can always place in the freezer if it is not stiffening up.)

Strawberry Whipped Cream

1 (14-oz [414-ml]) can coconut cream, refrigerated overnight or longer

5 Tbsp/50 g powdered sugar

2 Tbsp/30 ml strawberry Sweet Sauce (page 149), chilled

Open the can (do your best not to shake or vigorously move it). Scoop the top thick layer into a medium-sized deep bowl. If the cream has been chilled long enough, you can use the majority of the can's content—the beauty of using coconut cream.

Combine the powdered sugar and strawberry Sweet Sauce (chilled) with an electric mixer on medium speed until fluffy, 3 to 5 minutes. (You can always place in the freezer if it is not stiffening up.)

FROSTINGS & ICINGS

The frosting is really what makes a cake or cupcake attention grabbing and authoritative. Each frosting pairs with a treat from the cake chapter, but feel free to use the recipes as you will and allow your imagination to run with it.

FLUFFY DARK CHOCOLATE FROSTING

Pairs with the Blackout Cake (page 101).

FROSTS 12 CUPCAKES OR 1 TWO-LAYERED CAKE

2 ¾ c/330 g powdered sugar
½ c/44 g dark cocoa powder
½ c/112 g non-hydrogenated shortening
½ c/112 g vegan butter, softened
2 Tbsp/30 g melted chocolate, cooled
1 tsp vanilla extract
2 tsp nondairy milk

In a medium bowl, sift together the powdered sugar and cocoa powder.

In a mixing bowl, beat the shortening and vegan butter on medium speed with an electric mixer until fluffy, approximately 30 seconds. Beat in the melted chocolate until combined, then gradually add the sugar and cocoa mixture. Blend in the vanilla extract and nondairy milk until light and fluffy.

CINNAMON-SPICED BUTTERCREAM FROSTING

Pairs with the Gingerbread Cupcakes (page 93).

FROSTS 12 CUPCAKES OR 1 TWO-LAYERED CAKE

3 c/360 g powdered sugar
2 tsp/5 g cinnamon
½ tsp nutmeg
1 c/224 g vegan butter, softened
1 tsp vanilla extract
2 tsp nondairy milk

In a medium bowl, whisk together the powdered sugar, cinnamon and nutmeg.

In a mixing bowl, beat the vegan butter on medium speed with an electric mixer until fluffy, approximately 30 seconds. Gradually add the sugar, cinnamon and nutmeg mixture. Blend in the vanilla extract and nondairy milk until light and fluffy.

Cream Cheese Frosting

Pairs with the Pumpkin Cupcakes (page 99) and the Hangover Cure cake (page 105).

Frosts 12 cupcakes or 1 two-layered cake

¼ c/56 g vegan butter, softened
½ c/112 g vegan cream cheese
3 c/360 g powdered sugar
2 tsp nondairy milk
½ tsp vanilla extract

With an electric mixer, cream the vegan butter and cream cheese on medium speed until fluffy. Beat in the powdered sugar until fluffy. Add the milk and extract until just combined.

Lemon Drop Frosting

Pairs with the Lemonade Stand Cupcakes (page 100).

Frosts 12 cupcakes or 1 two-layered cake

1 c/224 g vegan butter, softened
3 c/360 g powdered sugar
2 tsp/10 ml lemon juice
¼ tsp vanilla extract
3 tsp/9.5 g lemon zest

With an electric mixer, cream the vegan butter on medium speed until fluffy. Gradually add in the powdered sugar and then beat in the lemon juice, extract and zest until light and fluffy.

Coconut-Dream Frosting

Pairs with the Whiteout Cake (page 106).

Frosts 12 cupcakes or 1 two-layered cake

¾ c/168 g vegan butter, softened

½ c/112 g non-hydrogenated shortening

3 c/360 g powdered sugar

3 tsp/15 ml canned coconut milk

½ c/30 g finely shredded coconut

1 tsp vanilla extract

With an electric mixer, cream the vegan butter and shortening on medium speed until fluffy. Gradually add in the powdered sugar, and then beat in the coconut milk. Add the shredded coconut and vanilla extract until light and fluffy.

Nutter Butter Frosting

Pairs with the Peanut Butter Chocolate Cupcakes (page 95).

Frosts 12 cupcakes or 1 two-layered cake

½ c/112 g vegan butter, softened

¼ c/65 g creamy peanut butter

3 c/360 g powdered sugar

3 Tbsp/45 ml nondairy milk

1 tsp vanilla extract

With an electric mixer, cream the vegan butter on medium speed until fluffy. Beat in the peanut butter, and then gradually add in the powdered sugar. Add the nondairy milk and vanilla extract until light and fluffy.

CARA'S TIP: If you desire, you can switch to almond butter for this recipe, or if you are allergic to nuts, you can use a nut-free spread like SunButter instead.

Coconut Walnut Icing

Pairs with the German Chocolate Cake (page 102).

Frosts 12 cupcakes or 1 two-layered cake

2 c/90 g shredded coconut
1 c/235 ml coconut milk
1 c/146 g lightly packed brown sugar
2 tsp vanilla extract
¼ c/60 ml unrefined coconut oil
1 ½ c/174 g finely chopped walnuts

Combine the first 5 ingredients in a small saucepan over low heat until the sugar has dissolved and thickened a bit, approximately 12 to 15 minutes, continuously stirring. Remove from the heat and add the coconut oil and walnuts. Allow to cool down and thicken up before spreading.

Simple Donut Icing

The perfect icing for 12 mini donuts or 6 large ones

1 ½ c/180 g powdered sugar
¼ c/60 ml unrefined coconut oil, melted
½ tsp vanilla extract
2 Tbsp/30 ml hot water

In a shallow bowl, combine the powdered sugar into the melted oil. Add vanilla extract and water until thick but thin enough to stir with ease. Add more water if too thick or more powdered sugar if too thin. Gently dip donuts (page 65) into the icing until tops are covered.

CARA'S TIP: For a chocolate glaze, add 2 tablespoons/ 30 ml melted chocolate and increase powdered sugar by 3 tablespoons/81 g.

Royal Icing

Use for the Gingerbread Men cookies (page 38).

Makes ½ cup/100 g of icing

1 c/120 g powdered sugar
¼ tsp vanilla extract
1 Tbsp/15 ml nondairy milk

In a small mixing bowl, combine powdered sugar and vanilla. Stir in a dash of nondairy milk until well blended and thick. If too thin, add more sugar by the teaspoon. If too thick, add another teaspoon dash of milk until desired consistency is achieved.

FOOD COLORINGS

Keep in mind that these all-natural (and by all-natural, I mean actually natural—not the kind of natural you read on processed junk) food colorings are pastels rather than bright colors when mixed in frostings or icings.

Pink

Creates ¼ cup/60 ml of food coloring

¼ c/62 g beets, canned
1 tsp beet juice from a can

In a high-speed blender, mix until smooth.

Add by the teaspoonful into icings, frostings or batter to give a pink hue.

In an airtight container, store in the refrigerator for up to 2 weeks.

Yellow

Creates ¼ cup/60 ml of food coloring

¼ c/60 ml water

½ tsp ground turmeric

In a small saucepan, boil both ingredients for 3 to 5 minutes. Allow to fully cool.

Add by the teaspoonful into icings, frostings or batter to give a yellow hue.

In an airtight container, store in the refrigerator for up to 2 weeks. Be careful, turmeric can stain, so use a container you don't mind turning yellow.

Purple

Creates ¼ cup/60 ml of food coloring

¼ c/35 g blueberries, fresh (or frozen, thawed and drained)

2 tsp water

In a high-speed blender, blend the blueberries and water together until completely smooth as can be. Using a fine-mesh sieve, strain the skins from the mix.

Add by the teaspoonful into icings, frostings or batter to give a purple hue.

In an airtight container, store in the refrigerator for up to 2 weeks.

Green

1 c/30 g fresh spinach (or frozen, thawed and drained)

3 Tbsp/45 ml water

In a small saucepan, boil the spinach and water for 5 minutes, covered (if you are using the frozen spinach, skip to the blending).

In a high-speed blender, blend the spinach and water together until completely smooth.

Add by the teaspoonful into icings, frostings or batter to give a green hue.

In an airtight container, store in the refrigerator for up to 2 weeks.

SPRINKLES

Sugar Glitter

Sugar Glitter is by far my favorite way to decorate my cakes and cupcakes. They add a simple elegance and sparkle that is just needed for that special dessert. My favorite part about these sprinkles? The pastel colors created by the food coloring, which make them look like they are crystals.

Creates ½ cup/50 g of sugar glitter

½ c/100 g coarse sugar

2 drops food coloring of choice (page 158)

Place in a plastic bag and shake until the color is fully blended in.

Spread on a parchment paper–lined baking sheet and allow to dry out for 2 to 3 hours. Keep stored in an airtight jar.

Rainbow Sprinkles

While some people at night might dream about their previous day, I dream about recipes. Is that weird? I literally wake up early in the morning to write down ideas that I've worked out in my sleep. The thought of these sprinkles originated on my website with a recipe for Candy Buttons, but in my slumber it occurred to me that I could totally transform these into sprinkles. Pastel-colored, super-adorable homemade sprinkles. I'm in love.

CREATES ½ CUP/35 G SPRINKLES

2 ½ c/300 g powdered sugar

3 tsp/9.5 g cornstarch

3 tsp/9.5 g Ener-G Egg Replacer plus 3 Tbsp/45 ml water

¼ tsp vanilla extract

¼ tsp almond extract

In a bowl, whisk together the sugar and cornstarch. Throw in the remaining ingredients and mix until a thick paste forms. This thick paste should not be runny—if it is, add more powdered sugar, 1 tablespoon/8 g at a time, until difficult to stir.

Line 2 baking sheets with a piece of parchment paper each.

You will need 5 small bowls (1 for each food coloring, plus 1 reserved for white sprinkles). Divide the paste evenly into each bowl, add a couple of drops of homemade food coloring (page 158) to each bowl and stir until color is fully blended in. Place each colored paste into either a plastic baggie with a very small slit cut in 1 of the corners or a squeeze bottle that has a small nozzle.

Gently squeeze parallel, very thin lines onto the baking sheet until you use up all of the colored paste. Allow to set out for 24 to 48 hours in a dry area. Once completely set, chop up with a knife and store in an airtight jar.

> CARA'S TIP: I know you are reading that last part and are thinking, ARE YOU OUT OF YOUR MIND? 24 to 48 hours? To that I say, yes, I am. That is beside the point, but, yes, I am serious about allowing it to set for that long—the longer the sprinkles sit out, the firmer they become.

Chocolate Sprinkles

Creates ½ cup/35 g sprinkles

2 ¼ c/270 g powdered sugar
½ c/44 g dark cocoa powder
3 tsp/9.5 g cornstarch
3 tsp/9.5 g Ener-G Egg Replacer plus
4 Tbsp/60 ml water
¼ tsp vanilla extract
¼ tsp almond extract

In a bowl, whisk together the sugar, cocoa and cornstarch. Throw in the remaining ingredients and mix until a thick paste has formed. This thick paste should not be runny—if it is, add more powdered sugar, 1 tablespoon/8 g at a time, until difficult to stir.

Line 2 baking sheets with a piece of parchment paper each.

Place into either a plastic baggie with a very small slit cut in 1 of the corners or a squeeze bottle that has a small nozzle. Gently squeeze parallel, thin lines onto the baking sheet until you use up all of the paste. Allow to set out for 24 to 48 hours in a dry area. Once completely set, chop up with a knife and store in an airtight jar.

Resources

There is a variety of tips and tricks to keep in mind when baking gluten-, egg- and dairy-free, which is why I have compiled this resource guide for you. My hope is that it will answer your questions about what type of egg substitutes are out there and how they properly work in a variety of recipes, how to substitute dairy in baking and even offer you a guide on how to create a gluten-free flour blend of your own. May it be of help to you as you begin this crazy journey of allergen-friendly baking!

You will see either my All-Purpose Blend or my Special Blend being used throughout the recipes in this book. Please refer back here for the exact measurements. You are always free to create your own gluten-free flour blend (page 171) but please keep in mind that the weight measurements in each recipe will look different if you do so.

Cara's All-Purpose Blend

This is the all-purpose blend I use for practically everything. It is perfect for substituting regular flour on a one-to-one basis.

Makes 9 cups/1498 g flour blend total

3 c/480 g superfine brown rice flour
3 c/538 g superfine sorghum flour
1 ½ c/288 g potato starch, not flour
1 ½ c/288 g arrowroot powder

With a spoon, scoop the flours into a measuring cup. Level with a knife and throw everything into a gallon-sized plastic baggie, seal tightly and shake vigorously until well combined. Keep stored in an airtight container.

Cara's Special Blend

If you can digest gluten-free certified oats, this is a really great special blend. It lends a nice flavor, texture and rise to baked goods. If you cannot digest oats or even millet, substitute with either brown rice flour or one of the medium weight flours listed on page 169, but keep in mind that the weight measurement will be different if you use flour not listed here.

Makes 9 cups/1123 g flour blend total

3 c/270 g gluten-free oat flour
3 c/357 g millet flour
2 c/240 g tapioca flour
1 c/192 g arrowroot powder

With a spoon, scoop the flours into a measuring cup. Level with a knife and throw everything into a gallon-sized/3.8-liter plastic baggie, seal tightly, and shake vigorously until well combined. Keep stored in an airtight container.

Making Your Own Gluten-Free Flour Blend

Unlike baking with regular gluten-filled flour, which just requires an all-purpose flour, gluten-free baking requires a fun, scientific blend of at least two flours. Now is the time to experiment to find out which blended flavors and textures fit your personal preferences. I have included what I have found to be the best results for myself (see page 166 for my two favorite blends), although I highly encourage you to figure out what works best for you.

If you want to branch out on your own, here is a helpful guide to deciding what to use. Ideally, you want a blend of two medium flours and at least one light flour choice, though feel free to expand on that. The more medium to heavy flours you use, the more varied the flavor and texture will be. Remember, the weight of each flour varies, so if you are going to sub in your own mix in a recipe, the weight measurement will be different from what is specified in the recipe. Experimenting is always key!

Light Flours

Tapioca Flour/Starch: Extracted from the cassava root, this starch is typically used as a thickening agent in recipes. Due to its binding abilities, it helps your gluten-free flour blend to be more cohesive. Tapioca also gives a nice crisp crust for your breads, improving the texture of your baked goods.

Potato Starch (not flour): Extracted from potatoes, this starch is also a great thickening agent that enables binding in your blend. Potato starch is a great flour to use to lend your baked goods moisture when needed. In gluten-free baking, this is one of my go-to starches. Can't tolerate nightshade foods, so potato starch is out? Not a problem! You can use arrowroot powder or tapioca starch instead.

Please note that there is potato starch and potato flour—these are not the same thing. If you are going to use potato starch, double-check the labels to make sure you did not accidently pick up the wrong product.

Arrowroot Powder: This easy to digest starch is extracted from a combination of several plant rootstocks. This is one of my favorites.

Cornstarch: Cornstarch can be a great option if you desire a crunchier crust in your recipe. Try using it with another starch for better results. Make sure to find an organic non-GMO brand if this is something that concerns you.

Medium Flours

Millet: With a dry and slightly nutty taste, millet is a predominantly starchy grain with a protein content similar to wheat flour. It's best to use millet in combination with other flours.

Quinoa: This flour gives a great rise to your baked goods; however, it has a distinct flavor that can at times be overpowering. This is a good flour to choose when using cocoa powder because by the time the item cools down, the quinoa flavor is slightly less noticeable.

Oat: Ground from oats, this flour is rich in fiber and vitamins. It gives great flavor to your baked goods and yields great results when combined with another medium flour. It can also be used as the only flour in your blend with starch(es).

Sorghum: This is another great substitute for wheat flour. It is one of my go-to medium flours for my all-purpose mix. It yields a light, moist baked good and pairs beautifully with other medium and heavy flours. It can also be used as the only flour in your blend with starch(es).

White Rice: You definitely want to combine this flour because it is notorious for yielding a gritty texture. (I have had great luck with white rice flour purchased from an Indian market because the rice is more finely ground.) Sweet white rice (also known as mochiko or glutinous rice, although it does not contain gluten) flour adds great moisture and binding and should be used in small portions in your mix.

Garbanzo Bean: This flour from the bean yields a nice rise in baked goods. Garbanzo bean flour, if you can get past its very distinct bean smell and flavor, will give you some of the best results in your gluten-free baked goods' rise. It can be used as the only flour in your blend with starch(es).

Fava Bean: This flour is usually found as a mix with garbanzo bean flour and yields a nice rise in baked goods. Keep in mind that it also yields a very distinct bean flavor.

Heavy Flours

Brown Rice: One of my favorite brands to use is Authentic Foods Superfine Brown Rice Flour because as it suggests, the superfine ground actually makes it grit-free. It is also one of the go-to flours in my all-purpose mix. It is a great substitute for wheat flour and works great when combined with a medium flour. It can also be used as the only flour in your blend with starch(es).

Buckwheat: Don't be fooled by the name; buckwheat is not derived from wheat but rather from a fruit. This flour works nicely on its own along with a light flour or in combination with other medium flours.

Almond or Cashew Flour: Low in carbs with a nice kick of protein, almond meal is a great way to give your baked goods a slight nutty flavor. If you are not allergic to nuts, try adding ¼ cup/21 g of this flour to your blend—it will help with binding and add overall moisture to your recipe.

Amaranth: Derived from the seeds of the amaranth plant, this stone-ground flour can be used alone for low rise baked goods or in combination with a mix of medium flours.

Teff: Teff is a nutritiously dense flour and should not be used alone. I really like to add a good ¼ cup/40 g to my all-purpose mix to give it a beautiful overall whole wheat color.

Corn: A hearty, dense flour, corn can be a great addition for your all-purpose mix, giving a good amount of binding and rise. It will, however, give a cornbread-like texture and flavor, so just be careful how much you add into your mix.

Coconut: A dense flour that should be combined with other medium flours, coconut needs to be used in smaller amounts because it has the tendency to take the moisture out of the batter. It is a great binder and provides moisture in the end result, so I suggest using only ¼ cup/28 g.

All-Purpose Flour Mix of Your Own

To create an all-purpose blend of your very own, keep in mind that you always want to use a combination of flours. The flavor and texture of your baked goods improve when you use more of the medium to heavy flours together. Here are four blending combinations you can follow to create your own flour mix:

How to create a Gluten-Free Blend

COMBO 1: 1 Medium Flour + 1 or 2 Starches

COMBO 2: 2 Medium Flour + 1 or 2 Starches

COMBO 3: 1 Medium Flour + 1 Heavy Flour + 1 or 2 Starches

COMBO 4: A variety of Medium and Heavy Flours of choice + 1 or 2 Starches

Keep in mind that you will need to add a gum to the overall recipe to mimic gluten, especially for your high-rise bread recipes. Xanthan and guar gums enable your baked goods to remain whole and not crumble.

Baking Without Eggs

The more you understand the purpose of egg substitutes and where they best work in your recipes, the better you will comprehend the world of baking without eggs. I use a variety of favorites, some of which are listed below. I have dabbled with all of these, but there are a few I am more experienced with because I have found more favorable results in the kitchen. You will find them listed in the ingredients of this book.

Ground Psyllium Husk: You can find this as a dietary supplement at your local health food store. When mixed in water, the ground psyllium husks begin to expand and become super gelatinous.

Chia Seed: You can use either white or black chia seeds, though might I suggest that if you are making a lighter-colored baked good to use the white. If you cannot find them locally, you can easily use the black seeds. It won't change the flavor; only create a darker hue to your recipe. Chia seeds, when added to water, create a wall of gel that is similar to eggs.

Flaxseed Meal: Just like the above ground psyllium husks and chia seeds, flaxseed meal has the same effect in water—it expands and becomes gel-like. It's a great substitution for the viscosity of eggs.

Egg Powder Replacer: I particularly like Ener-G Egg Replacer. For me, it is one of the best egg replacers out there. Buy it if you are able to find it at your local health food store or online. It is simply a strategic mix of starches that creates beautiful results in your baked goods.

Fruit & Veggie Purée: Applesauce, pumpkin purée and sweet potato purée are examples of fruit and veggie purées. These are great binders and a low-fat, nutritious way to create an egg substitute. They also inject moisture into your goods, which is always a plus.

Tofu, Nondairy Yogurts & Eggless Mayo: One of the great aspects of these egg substitutes is the high amount of fat they contain, which when baking gluten-free and vegan is an extremely helpful quality to have for binding and rise.

Baking Soda & Vinegar (or Lemon Juice): I particularly love using apple cider vinegar in this, another one of my favorite egg substitutes. The two merged together create a science experiment of explosion in your recipe, which causes your baked goods to rise nicely. Please note that if you cannot digest vinegar, you may substitute with lemon juice.

Each item listed below is an easy go-to measurement for replacing one egg in a recipe. If the recipe calls for two eggs, simply double the amount. Please note that not every item listed should be substituted in every situation. Part of the journey is researching and having an appetite for knowledge. It's empowering, I promise, despite how overwhelming it may seem. Get to know these items and start experimenting in your own kitchen. Your tastes might be different from mine, and that is the beauty of individuality.

Use the following for 1 egg

- 1 ½ teaspoons/4 g Ener-G + 3 tablespoons/45 ml Water
- ¼ cup/61 g Applesauce
- 1 tablespoon/6 g Ground Chai + 3 tablespoons/45 ml Water
- ¼ cup/60 g Nondairy Yogurt
- 1 tablespoon/15 ml Vinegar + ½ teaspoon Baking Soda
- ¼ cup/56 g Mashed Banana
- ¼ cup/60 g Purée (Pumpkin, Sweet Potato, etc.)
- 1 tablespoon/15 g Flax Meal + 3 tablespoons/45 ml Water
- ¼ cup/60 g Blended Silken Tofu
- ¼ cup/60 g Eggless Mayo
- 1 tablespoon/15 g Psyllium + 3 tablespoons/45 ml Water

Each item has its own purpose and role in a certain type of baked good. For example, if I am looking for a crunchier cookie, I am going to opt for an item that will harden the cookie, like a starch (think egg replacement powder like Ener-G). If I am trying to create a chewier cookie, I would opt for a fruit purée like applesauce or even pumpkin purée since these create a moist, tender bite.

For cakes, I would look to an egg replacement powder like Ener-G, "buttermilk" mixed with baking soda, or flaxseed meal or even chia seeds. Again, this is personal preference. Here is what I have found to work best in certain types of baked goods:

Cakes, muffins, quick breads

- Ener-G Egg Replacer
- Chia Seeds
- "Buttermilk": Vinegar + Nondairy Milk
- Fruit/Veggie Purée
- Nondairy Mayo or Yogurt
- Applesauce

Cookies, brownies, Bars

- Ener-G Egg Replacer
- Flaxseed Meal
- Tofu
- Fruit Purée

Yeast Breads

- Chia Seeds
- Psyllium
- Veggie Purée
- Ener-G Egg Replacer

Egg Wash

1 teaspoon Cornstarch +
1 tablespoon/15 ml Water, whisked

If you see an egg replacer in one of my recipes that you want to change, feel free to do so! How else will you know what works best for you unless you experiment? Just please understand that if you alter any of the ingredients, I cannot guarantee the same results.

Baking Without Dairy

Milk substitutions are very simple to find. You have several choices, including coconut, rice, soy, oat, hemp and all nut and seed options. Part of your choice will be dependent upon personal preference and taste; the other part will be dependent upon the desired results in your baked goods. The rule of thumb is the more fat in the nondairy milk, the better the baked goods. Not only does fat help with texture and flavor, it also helps with rise (and you need all the help you can get with gluten- and egg-free baking). This is why you will see coconut milk in a lot of my recipes. If you cannot have coconut (or do not like it), simply replace with a nondairy milk of your choice. Easy, right?

Use the Following for Milk

- Store-Bought Nut Milks
- Homemade Nut Milks
- Rice, Soy, Oat or Hemp Milk
- Coconut Milk (canned or So Delicious)

Use the Following for Whipped Cream

- Homemade from Coconut Milk
- Store-Bought Nondairy
- Homemade from Nuts

Use the Following for Heavy Cream

For Savory:
- Cashew "Cream"
- White Bean Purée
- Avocado
- Cauliflower, Potato or Squash Purée
- Canned Coconut Milk

For Sweet Goods:
- Canned Coconut Milk
- Nondairy Creamer

Sweet & Whipped Cream

Sweet creams require a little more creativity. Think of foods that have a naturally creamy taste that also blend well. Narrow it down to a variety of nuts (e.g., cashews, macadamias, etc.) and coconut milk. You will be surprised by how creamy a cashew cream can be. Note that almonds, Brazil nuts and even pistachios can work here too. Allergic to nuts? Give sunflower cream a shot!

Butter

There are a good number of store-bought butter substitutes that can be used in baked goods. A recipe heavy in butter may sometimes yield different results (e.g., cookies might spread when the recipe calls for the cookies to keep their shape). Earth Balance carries a good butter alternative that tastes great spread over a slice of gluten-free bread or even when used in sautéing or baking. It is made from various oils, including soy. Avoiding soy? There is a soy-free version too! Coconut oil is also a good substitute. Be sure to get the unrefined version if you do not like the flavor of coconut.

USE THE FOLLOWING FOR Butter

- Nondairy Butter (e.g., Earth Balance or Fleischmann's)
- Homemade from Coconut
- Shortening
- Coconut Oil
- Oils (Olive, Vegetable, Canola, etc.)
- Applesauce

Cheese

For the sake of baking, I stick to store-bought vegan cheeses—see my Cheez-It recipe (page 24). I find it to be very forgiving in baked goods. If you want to get creative for those savory baked goods, consider a butternut squash purée with a pinch of cheesy nutritional yeast.

USE THE FOLLOWING FOR Cheese

- Store-bought Vegan Shredded Cheese
- Squash Purée
- Cashews/Nuts
- Nutritional Yeast

Cream Cheese & Yogurt

I find that there are some great choices for cream cheese and yogurt substitutes at the store. Some do have different tastes to them according to what their bases are (soy, coconut, etc.), so what you decide to go with will be based on personal preference. If you have the time and are feeling up to it, there are plenty of homemade recipes out there as well.

USE THE FOLLOWING FOR SOUR CREAM/ CREAM CHEESE

- Store-Bought (e.g., So Delicious brand)
- Homemade from Tofu
- Homemade from Nuts

USE THE FOLLOWING FOR HEAVY CREAM

- Store-Bought (e.g., So Delicious brand)
- Homemade from Nondairy Milk

BAKING TIPS & TRICKS

To help your experience in the kitchen become a less stressful one, I have several tips on what to expect when baking without the gluten, eggs and dairy to share with you.

Sticky Dough: Keep in mind that gluten-free and vegan dough tends to be slightly sticky. Always handle dough with either wet fingers, lightly floured hands or use wax or parchment paper to ensure that it doesn't stick to your fingers.

Rolling Out Dough: Always roll your dough between two pieces of parchment paper. This will greatly help your sanity and keep the dough from sticking to the counter or rolling pin. If you are still having troubles, place the dough in the fridge to chill for at least 30 minutes.

Crumbly Dough: If your dough becomes crumbly throughout the course of being chilled or even when sitting out on the counter, add 1 teaspoon of water at a time to rehydrate. Before adding more, make sure that the water is thoroughly blending in. Also, if you play around with and knead the dough, the warmth of your hands can be enough to make it more cohesive.

Inconsistent Batters: Don't compare gluten-free and vegan batters to regular ones. Gluten-free and vegan batters tend to be a little runnier than regular batter and not as firm (e.g., the batter for the Cinnamon Raisin Loaf is more of a spoonable batter than what a typical bread dough would be).

Fats: The more fat in the nondairy (butter or milk) substitute, the better! Fat helps greatly with the overall flavor and texture in your baked goods. This is why I use coconut milk in a lot of my recipes. If you do not like the flavor or are allergic, just try to find a nondairy substitute with a high amount of fat.

Oven Temperatures: Please check your oven temperature to make sure that it is accurate. This will greatly help with creating an evenly baked product; otherwise you will have a firm crust on the outside and a gummy center.

Baking Time: Most gluten-free goods need to be baked longer because the batter and dough tend to be moister than regular batters. If you are taking a loved recipe and converting it on your own, make sure you give it a little more baking time.

Higher Altitudes: The higher you are above sea level, the more changes you will need to make in baking temperatures, times and even in the amount of moisture in the ingredients. Please research the proper settings needed for your high-altitude location.

Substituting Ingredients: Feel free to substitute whatever you desire (pages 171-178 give you a wide variety of the different substitutions that are out there), but please note that when you change the recipe, there is no guarantee that the overall baked good will have the same results.

Baking Pans: Due to the finicky nature of these baked goods, make sure that you are using thick and sturdy pans to bake in. Avoid the thin, flimsy pans—they will not bake evenly and will cook the outsides too fast, leaving the middles gummy.

Cooling Period: Do not allow the goods to fully cool in their pans (unless specified). If you do, they become soggy. Always cool these baked goods for a brief time in their pans until it is easy to touch them, then transfer them to a wire rack. Also, allowing the goods to fully cool ensures that they will not only solidify and not be crumbly, but will not be gummy on the inside as well.

Storage: Always store your baked goods in an airtight container after they have cooled, and store them either in the refrigerator or freezer. Remember that they do not store as long as typical baked goods and taste best if devoured the day they're baked.

Do you have more questions on gluten-free/vegan substitutions? Visit my website www.forkandbeans.com to learn more or even ask a question. I'd love to hear from you!

ACKNOWLEDGMENTS

Thank you to Page Street Publishing for helping make my first cookbook writing experience such a great one.

To Matt, who watched me go through every emotion throughout this entire process . . . and still loves me, you are not only the reason I am able to pursue my passion in this field, but you are also the greatest gift I have ever been given.

My eternal gratitude to my testers, Dawn Simpson, Jennifer Miller, Brooke Idol, Kiersten Frase, Hayley Ryczek, Kelly Cavalier and Celine Steen. Thank you for lending your kitchens, advice and gentleness to help me out.

Laurel VanBlarcum, your generosity to help with editing blows me away. You have been such a great friend to me in the past two years and have been so thoughtful with your advice, guidance and encouragement along the way.

To my family—my mom (my biggest fan), Dave, my dad (see, I'm finally a productive member of society!), Lynne, the Keith Family: Sherry, Bobert, Cambria, CoCo and Cara Jr.—you girls are why I create these recipes, the Meyers: Scott (my future manager), Heather, Kennedy, Reyn and Katrina.

To my friends—Rose, Sumer, Brooke, Fanny and Blondie. Thank you for not being mad at me for being quiet while I went into a cave to finish this beast.

To my very special Jan—without your guidance, compassion and unwavering encouragement, I'm not sure I would have gotten through this. Thank you, Coach! Your friendship means the world to me.

To Celine Steen—your talent and photos are incredible but not as great as your heart. Thank you for your friendship and guidance—I couldn't have asked for a better photographer.

To Kathy Hester—you are the reason this book exists.

To my readers and the friends I have made along the road of blogging—you are the other reason this book exists. Thank you for the support and love over the past two years.

ABOUT THE AUTHOR

Cara Reed is the face behind the popular website www.forkandbeans.com—a place where you can find all recipes creatively gluten-, egg- and dairy-free. It is her personal mission to understand and conquer allergy-safe baking because in her opinion, no one should ever have to skimp on the fun of eating simply because they must avoid certain foods. She lives in Los Angeles, California.

INDEX